ESSAYS IN HANSEATIC HISTORY

Trinity Guild Hall as it appeared in the 15th century

Essays in Hanseatic History

THE KING'S LYNN SYMPOSIUM
1998

EDITORS

Klaus Friedland and Paul Richards

Larks Press

Published by the Larks Press
Ordnance Farmhouse, Guist Bottom, Dereham,
Norfolk NR20 5PF
01328 829207
Larks.Press@btinternet.com
Website: www.booksatlarkspress.co.uk

Printed by Newprint and Design,
Garrood Drive, Fakenham, Norfolk

First published September 2005
Reprinted 2009

British Library Cataloguing-in-Publication Data
A catalogue record for this book is available
from the British Library

ACKNOWLEDGEMENTS

The Mayor of King's Lynn and West Norfolk invited the Hanseatic History Union
to King's Lynn in June 1998 and the Council and its officers, along with the staff
at the Town Hall, offered full support and splendid hospitality. This book has its
origins in the Symposium held in the medieval Trinity Guildhall,
now the Town Hall.
Rosemary Bryan typed the final draft of the book and has been most helpful to the
editors. The editors would also like to thank Susan Yaxley of the Larks Press for
her hard work and commitment to the project.
This publication has been made possible through the assistance of the Hanseatic
History Union whose officers and members so much enjoyed their visit to
King's Lynn in 1998.

ISBN 978 1 904006 29 9

CONTENTS

ILLUSTRATIONS

Preface

As important in the Middle Ages as Liverpool was to become in the Industrial Revolution, Lynn was a major English seaport for several centuries, with river access to a wide hinterland and facing Europe across the North Sea. Coastal trade with London and Northern Britain was significant too. Aptly described by a leading historian as 'the Warehouse on the Wash', that large bay on England's east coast, the town retained some maritime prominence until the railways robbed it of both river and sea traffic after 1850. But the Port of Lynn had reached its international zenith between 1250 and 1500 when commercial intercourse with the cities of the German Hanse loomed large for this Norfolk borough.

The interest of local historians in Lynn's association with the German Hanse has long been stimulated by a complex of buildings spanning the 15th to 18th centuries by the River Great Ouse. This is known today as St Margaret's House but was once a Hanseatic Steelyard or Warehouse. It remained in the possession of 'The Hans Towns' of Lübeck, Hamburg and Bremen until 1751 when the property was sold to a Lynn merchant for £800. Described in documents before 1751 as 'Allemayne Mansion' or the 'Stillyard House', this historic complex has been subject to some alteration since the 1470s, but is still the sole surviving Hanseatic Steelyard in England. To complement this architectural evidence of Lynn's significance to the Hanseatic League there is the Borough Archive at the nearby Town Hall. Here can be found fascinating material telling of the politics and commerce linking the Wash harbour to Baltic cities in the 14th and 15th centuries.

Mr Syd Swan of Aldeburgh in Suffolk introduced me to the Hanseatic History Society in 1991. We decided to lobby Lübeck for one of its occasional international symposia to come to Lynn and our proposal received a favourable response in 1994. The turning point arrived in 1997 when Professor Klaus Friedland travelled to England to explore this Wash seaport. To our delight he found Lynn an ideal location for a Symposium of the Hanseatic History Society and suggested June 1998. In August 1997 Dr Stuart Jenks was the guest speaker at the annual lecture of the Civic Society in Lynn. Not only did he talk enthusiastically about Lynn and the Hanseatic League to a large audience in the Town Hall, but was obviously ready to return in 1998.

I undertook my first journey to Lübeck in October 1997. Bürgermeister Michael Bouteiller welcomed us and encouraged Lynn to make the most of its Hanseatic connections; Dr Antjekathrin Grassmann showed us the treasures of the City Archive; Dr Rolf Hammel-Kiesow acted as an excellent guide around Lübeck's buildings and streets and Professor Klaus Friedland confirmed plans for a Lynn Symposium of the Hanseatic History Society. This was to take place in June 1998 at the invitation of the Mayor and Borough Council of King's Lynn and West Norfolk. I am indebted to Councillor Clifford Walters (Mayor 1997/98) for his agreement and permission.

During the winter of 1997/98 I worked with councillors and officers of the Borough Council on the arrangements for the visit of the Hanseatic History Society. We wished to extend public participation by including supporting events for the Lynn Symposium in a programme called 'Lynn's Hanse Days, 4 -7 June 1998'. I am grateful to those people in the Town Hall and the Tourism and Leisure Department in particular for their contributions to this project. Having been elected Mayor in early May 1998, I had the privilege of hosting 'Lynn's Hanse Days' and greeting delegates to the Symposium from home and abroad.

The Town Hall (a medieval guildhall with major later additions) was the venue for the Lynn Symposium which was opened on 4 June 1998 by the Mayor and Professor Klaus Friedland. Two of the sessions were public lectures (by Professor Walter Salmen and Dr Stuart Jenks). Two exhibitions were also accommodated here. The Norfolk Record Office mounted 'With Goods and Ships and Merchandise' using local records to illustrate Lynn's commercial and political relations with the German Hanse. 'Discover England's Hanseatic Heritage' was displayed by courtesy of the East of England Hanse partnership, a consortium of East Anglian towns and the regional Tourist Board. Opposite the Town Hall, across the Saturday Market Place, is St Margaret's Church where, on the evening of 5 June, Mr Aubrey Hood played the Snetzler organ for a large audience giving short talks to introduce the music of Buxtehude, Bohm and J.S. Bach. There were also daily town tours by the King's Lynn Town Guides with Hanseatic History their talking point.

Facing St Margaret's Church is the town's Hanseatic Steelyard or Warehouse, which was a focus of interest and activity for delegates to the Lynn Symposium. The German Embassy in London had also generously agreed to sponsor a new plaque for the courtyard of this historic complex to commemorate Lynn's close association with the Hanseatic League. His Excellency, Herr Gerbardt von Moltke, travelled from London to unveil the plaque after attending a luncheon at the Town Hall. His presence in the town at this time was appreciated by all. The liaison with the German Embassy had been in the hands of the Honorary Consul for the Federal Republic of Germany in Lynn, Mr David Hume, whose assistance to the Mayor was invaluable.

The Hanseatic Steelyard at King's Lynn from the east. The complex was redeveloped after 1475 when the Utrecht Treaty gave the Germans the ownership of this waterside site.

Delegates to the Lynn Symposium were glad of the opportunity to visit Boston, about 40 miles distant on the other corner of the Wash. Boston's Mayor guided us around the town. Boston had been an important English destination for Hanseatic merchants from the 13th century; there is a fine medieval memorial brass to one of them in the parish church, though their Warehouse or Steelyard no longer exists. On return from Boston to Lynn, a civic supper in the Town Hall ended 'Lynn's Hanse Days'.

'Lynn's Hanse Days' (4-6 June 1998) generated a great deal of local and regional attention and support whilst public events were well attended. The role of the town in English and Hanseatic History was recognised and celebrated, thus fostering civic pride and confidence for the future. These Hanse Days were, moreover, an excellent example of how international co-operation and understanding across Europe can be developed. None of this would have been possible without the Hanseatic History Society. I thank Professor Klaus Friedland and his fellow Englandfahrer.

Dr Paul Richards
September 1999

Mayor, Borough of King's Lynn and West Norfolk

7

Introduction

by

Klaus Friedland

The history of the Hanse has been professionally investigated for approximately one and a half centuries and, in these decades, has been seen as a free trade community without any constitutional arrangements. Some scholars have tried to comprehend it as a cartel. A highly efficient cartel, as far as supply and demand in late medieval northern Europe is concerned. Membership of the Hanse was granted to nearly two hundred towns in what are now France, Belgium, Netherlands, Denmark, Sweden, Estonia, Poland, Russia and, mainly, Northern Germany. Their business was particularly in foreign trade, with Norway (via the 'kontor' or factory at Bergen), with Russia (Novgorod), Netherlands (Brüges) and England (London, Lynn, Boston).

Symposia or exchanges of research and evidence have been held in Bergen (1970), London (1974), Visby (1984), Brüges (1988), Novgorod (1992)[1] and Lynn (1998).

Following an invitation by the Mayor of King's Lynn and West Norfolk, Dr Paul Richards, 30 participants attended the Symposium in King's Lynn from June 4 to June 7, 1998. This was most gratefully accepted as the town promised some, and possibly unique, constitutional evidence of the almost constitution-less Hanse community: one of the earliest Hanse aldermen acted in 1271 as an official representative of some sort of Hanse merchants' union to English kings.[2] In King's Lynn, at the same time, a Hanse kontor-building (St Margaret's House today) has been preserved almost in its original state, again a most singular case.

Participants enjoyed an organ concert in St Margaret's Church performed and commented on by Aubrey Hood, in connection with the Buxtehude tradition, a sea and harbour trip on the River Great Ouse and an excursion to Boston, once closely associated with Hanseatic and Norwegian trade.

The Symposium was concluded by the unveiling of a plaque at the old 'Steelyard' building by the Ambassador of the Federal Republic of Germany, His Excellency Gebhardt von Moltke, followed by a supper party in the Guildhall of the Holy Trinity.

Notes

[1] Published Quellen und Darstellungen zur Hansischen Geschichte Bände XVII (1971), XXIII (1976), XXXII (1987), XXXVI (1999), LII (2002).
[2] Cf.p.14

An aerial view of the Saturday Market Place, King's Lynn, showing the medieval quadrangular complexes of Hampton Court (top left), Hanseatic Steelyard with Georgian façade (adjacent) and Thoresby College (top middle right). The long building immediately below the latter is the Trinity Guildhall and Assembly Rooms (1421 and 1766 respectively). St Margaret's Church dominates. *Photo: Lynn News*

TOWN AND HARBOUR

The Hinterland and Overseas Trade of King's Lynn 1205 - 1537: an Introduction

by

Paul Richards

1. Bishop's Lynn in 1205

By the early 13th century Lynn had become a significant market town and seaport, having grown rapidly since 1101 when Bishop Losinga of Norwich recognised it as a settlement by the waterside on the western edge of his Gaywood estate. He had endowed the Benedictine monks of Norwich Cathedral with the lordship. Their Priory Church of St Margaret was, nevertheless, only to be built and rebuilt through the wealth of Lynn's mercantile community, though the Norwich bishops were determined to retain their grip on local power. They had founded a second town and market in the 1140s on the Newland to the north of the first and assumed the lordship of both centres – of Bishop's Lynn – in 1205.

In 1203/04 King John imposed a duty of a fifteenth on all imports and exports of seaborne trade (excepting coastal trade) and the results are recorded on the Pipe Roll. Though Bristol and Chester, amongst other west coast seaports, were not included in this fund-raising exercise, the totals indicate the relative importance of English harbours. London, not surprisingly, is handling the biggest volume of trade, but Boston, Southampton, Lincoln and Lynn come next in the taxation paid to the Crown. (The period of taxation was from July 1203 to November 1204).

Further evidence of the early commercial prominence of Lynn is the settlement of Jewish traders by the 1180s, but a pogrom in 1189 destroyed this group. Soldiers or sailors en route for the Crusade were amongst those blamed.

In 1205 there were 46 royal galleys stationed around the English coastal ports, from the Wash to the Severn, including Bishop's Lynn. This is another indicator of the high ranking of its harbour.[1]

That Lynn had qualified for official urban status was confirmed in 1204 when King John granted a charter making the town a free borough (granting trading privileges nationwide) and creating a gild merchant for the regulation of local trade.

This was followed in 1205 by a charter from John de Grey, King John's close friend and Bishop of Norwich, granting to the same community all the liberties enjoyed by the men of Oxford.

Lynn enjoyed limited independence from the Norwich bishops. There followed a long and bitter power struggle between local merchants and their ecclesiastical lords 45 miles to the east, though the latter built a palace at Gaywood, a mere 6 miles away, to where new mayors had to journey for approval. One concludes that Bishop de Grey was asserting rather than relinquishing his authority in his political manoeuvres of 1204/05. His stewards and officials managed Lynn's two law courts (one in each market place) and opened the two annual summer fairs (again in each market place).[2]

2. Lynn's Hinterland

Today, the river Great Ouse flows to the sea through Lynn, draining a large area of central England and Fenland. This was not always so. The rivers Nene and Ouse had meandering courses and found their way to the Wash at Wisbech, about 12 miles from Lynn. By 1250 the Wisbech estuary was badly silted up and artificial cuts were made to avoid it. The Well Creek redirected water from Outwell near Wisbech to enter the sea at Lynn; then the eastern branch of the Ouse was diverted by Brandon Creek to Littleport to flow towards the same Lynn estuary of the rivers Gay and Nar.[3]

Lynn's hinterland before the making of the above canals or cuts might appear to have been restricted, but both the Nene and Ouse had already been accessible from its harbour, probably via other routes. In 1169 there were royal arrangements for hiring boats between Cambridge and Lynn. Corn was being shipped along Fenland waterways to Lynn from Ely and Huntingdon by 1170. Lead was carried from Derbyshire along the same rivers in 1184 to reach London coastwise. In 1227 and 1274 Huntingdon men complained that their market was in danger from that of the Abbot of Ramsey at St Ives which was easier to access from Lynn.[4] Wine and provisions were despatched from the town's quays for the King's army at the siege of Kenilworth near Coventry in 1266.

Huge amounts of corn, wool, hides and ale were transported by water from several counties to Lynn. Wine, fish, salt, cloth and building materials were returned up river by its traders who regularly visited inland ports like St Ives and Ely. The estates of the Bishops of Ely constituted an inland economy of some size and dynamism by 1200. Produce was carted overland from their many manors to London but river connections with Lynn were equally important as the development of a waterside complex at Ely tells. Annual fairs at Lynn, Boston, Stamford, Northampton, St Ives and other

11

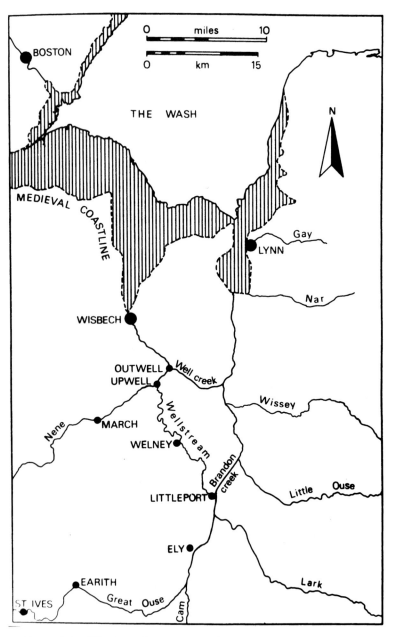

The coastline of the Wash and the Fenland rivers following the silting of the Wisbech estuary and diversion of the Great Ouse about 1250.

Society for Medieval Archaeology

places allowed merchants from home and abroad to seek bargains, all taking advantage of the commercial liberties offered at these events. Braudel reminds us how big fairs could mobilise the economy of an entire region with the business communities of Western Europe meeting to deal in wool, cloth, fish, furs and many other commodities.[5]

It seems that the diversion of the Ouse from Wisbech to Lynn some time before 1300 benefited the Wash port by extending its hinterland still further. Brandon Creek allowed the Great Ouse to meet the Little Ouse and River Wissey to the north-east thus opening a more direct route for the combined streams to Lynn. With the decline of the Wisbech outfall the traffic along the Well Creek increased and by 1300 it had become an important water highway between Lynn and the midland counties. In 1331 there was an obstruction at Outwell which interfered with navigation from Peterborough via March to the Norfolk port. Boats had to be diverted south to Littleport and hence along the Ouse to Lynn 'whereby grain, timber, wool, reed, turf, stone and other commodities were the dearer' as well as 'fish, herring and victuals'.[6] The obstruction was soon removed.

Further evidence of Lynn's broad hinterland is demonstrated by the petitioning to parliament by landowners in 1373 that the town should be a staple port due to the fact that 'various streams ran through the counties of Warwick, Leicester, Northampton, Rutland, Bedford, Buckingham, Huntingdon and Cambridge' by which wool and other commodities could 'be conveyed more easily and cheaply to Lynn than to any other port'.[7] It was granted. Lynn's commercial ties with the City of Cambridge were very close, but relations were sometimes acrimonious because of disagreements over the trading rights of local merchants in the other town. Lynn and Cambridge men remained united in their opposition to Fenland drainage schemes which threatened navigation and the regular traffic on the Ouse and its tributaries.

Hoskins says that the Great Ouse was probably the second largest river system in England by 1500, if not the first, because with its navigable tributaries it drained at least eight counties, all amongst England's richest. He reminds us of a writer in the time of Edward IV who spoke of it as 'the milky way, by reason of those accommodations of merchandise, food, and necessary provision, which are constantly carried up and down it; and Lynn sits at the door of this river, as it were the turnkey of it'.[8] The Great Ouse itself was navigable to Bedford for ships of fifteen tons. Wine, fish, salt, corn and coal were the main cargoes of the Fenland lighters. River traffic increased every September as Stourbridge Fair near Cambridge attracted thousands of traders and dealers seeking hops, wine, cheese, cloth and Baltic goods in particular. It was still an annual event of national standing in 1722 when Defoe marvelled at its size. He was equally impressed by the fact that Lynn enjoyed 'the greatest extent' of inland navigation of any English port

13

outside London and served six counties 'wholly' and three 'in part' with coal, wine and provisions.[9]

Historians have properly emphasised the rural and agricultural nature of Lynn's hinterland (after and before 1537), thus the impact of the annual harvest on its fortunes has been critical, the town having been a major English granary and corn exporter for centuries. But the remarkably profitable export of wool through Lynn and Boston dwindled in the course of the 15th century.

Parker says that Lynn was most prosperous, relative to other English towns, in the 13th century. Taxation records show that it had slipped to eleventh most important or wealthy town by 1334, but the post Black Death poll tax of 1377 sees Lynn rise to seventh; this position was maintained into the 16th century.[10] By 1600 the coastal traffic in corn and coal figured ever larger in keeping the commercial wheels of this Norfolk seaport turning as its role in international trade diminished. The town failed to develop any major industries, apart from the brewing and shipbuilding springing from its maritime economy. Its urban fabric was improved and remade between 1500 and 1700 but Lynn's expansion was modest.

3. Medieval Trade Overseas: Lynn

Lynn's prominence amongst English seaports in the Middle Ages depended on the extensive hinterland captured by the Great Ouse and its tributaries. It included several counties at the heart of the nation. Even though the expansion of the European economy was brought to an abrupt halt by the Black Death of 1348/49, with severe population losses and contraction of the cultivated area, the Wash port remained in a privileged geographical position. This was reinforced by its location on England's east coast, facing Europe across the North Sea, with London and Scotland within relatively easy reach. Lynn's centrality to England's overseas trade seems confirmed by the early local settlement of traders from Scandinavia, Germany, France, Flanders and Spain.

What was the character of Lynn's overseas trade in the Middle Ages?[11]

Friedland has discussed the growth in 'food supply and demand' in medieval northern Europe, including the leading role of the English.[12] Lynn was at the forefront of corn export. The Archbishop of Trondjheim was given permission by Henry II to buy grain from the Norfolk seaport even in times of scarcity. Once, about 1254, eleven Norwegian ships were loading corn in its harbour. Grain was also an important bulk cargo from Lynn to Flemish and French seaports for rising urban populations on the continent. In the middle decades of the 14th century Lynn men were frequently commissioned by the Crown to ship foodstuffs to armies in Scotland and

France; the local Melchbourne brothers were amongst England's top merchant capitalists, heavily committed to this traffic. Baltic grain was competing with English supplies by 1300, in Norway and Flanders especially and, in years of bad harvests, German corn came to England. Corn exports from Lynn continued, however, from the 12th through to the late 18th century when home consumption absorbed the English harvest. (Baltic grain was being imported into Lynn in greater quantities from the 1770s.)[13]

Salt was produced around the Wash from the 11th century (or earlier) with sea water evaporated in large pans. Population growth must have greatly increased the demand for this preservative of the fish so common to the diet of medieval Europeans. Ships from Norway, Denmark, Flanders and Germany were coming to Boston and Lynn for salt before 1200, though its more efficient production in warmer southern Europe led to the decline of the Wash industry. In the 14th century salt from the Bay of Bourgneuf was being exported to Lynn and Boston by the Dutch who took wool to France. *La Redcogge* of Lynn sailed twice to the Bay in 1363 to buy salt.[14] Scottish ships brought salt to Lynn too, increasingly by the 16th century (Lynn and its hinterland needed it primarily for domestic use).

Fish was a vital ingredient in the diet of medieval communities (for proteins) and the seas off Norway and the southern Baltic were teeming with cod and herring. In about 1250, Matthew Paris wondered at the 200 or more ships at Bergen. Here was the biggest fish market in Europe. Lynn ships taking corn and cloth to Norway before 1300 returned with timber, furs, hunting birds and fish. In the course of the 13th century the German Hanse took a firm grip on the fish trade of northern Europe, both in Bergen and the Baltic. Herring was being brought to Lynn and Hull in German ships in increasing amounts by the 1320s. Salt, fish and cloth were transported to Lynn by Scottish boats whose owners took home wheat, malt and ale. Dried and salted fish purchased in enormous quantities at Lynn's two annual fairs or marts was sent inland in barrels.

The harbours of Boston and Lynn were the destinations of numerous English ships carrying wine from Gascony where the vineyard had almost ousted the cornfield. It is estimated that five million gallons a year were being imported by the English in about 1300. Between September 1308 and June 1309 at least twenty-two vessels, laden with an average of 93 tons of wine, departed from the new Gascon port of Libourne for Lynn. In 1333/34, Lynn merchants chartered eleven ships to bring wine from France. In 1342 William Melchbourne was appointed deputy butler at Lynn to collect the two shillings per ton and twelve pence per pipe due to the King on all wine imports.[15] This lucrative trade was badly damaged during the Hundred Years' War (c1340-1450) between England and France; Gascon vineyards

15

were destroyed in the fighting and pirates attacked ships (despite the convoy system). Lulls in this long international conflict allowed some commercial activity. In 1362 Bordeaux wine merchants chartered the *Grace of God* of Lynn. Wine imports into Boston and Lynn declined in the 15th century because of the impact of warfare and the tightening hold of London merchants on the trade. French wine was, however, being imported into Lynn in the 16th century, apparently in a commercial revival. Shipmasters informed the government in 1583 that it was in the French wine trade that the 'cheifist parte of the merchantes lyvinges of that towne consisteth'.[16]

During the 12th and 13th centuries both Boston and Lynn exported huge amounts of wool to feed the looms of continental Europe, above all in industrial Flanders. French, German, Spanish, Italian and Flemish merchants frequented the annual fairs of the eastern counties searching for the best fleeces. By the 1280s, Boston was probably accounting for one third of total English wool exports, or 10,000 sacks a year. Its hinterland included England's largest and highest quality flocks. The Lincolnshire town was, however, the most vulnerable to the changes in the wool trade occurring in the 14th century when exports declined as more of the home crop was taken by the English cloth industry. This was partly the result of the taxation policies of the English kings from Edward I who saw wool exports as rich pickings in their fund-raising schemes for wars against the Welsh, Scottish and French. Crown interference in the flow of English wool to the continent was therefore partly responsible for the damage done to the trade of the Wash ports. In 1343, Thomas Melchbourne of Lynn was directed to ship, from Yarmouth to the staple in Flanders, all the wool he had collected in Norfolk on the King's behalf, and there to sell the same for his monarch. Lynn enjoyed a revival of wool exports in the 1380s when German ships were visiting the Wash harbour, but the trade contracts thereafter.

Stamford, Northampton, Lincoln and Leicester were centres for the manufacture of good quality cloth before 1300. Boston and Lynn were both well situated to export it. Their merchants acquired cloth at the regional fairs, along with Italian, Norwegian, French and Spanish men. Scarlets and greens were highly regarded colours in continental cities and royal courts. An indicator of the significance of the cloth producing hinterland of the Wash ports is the import of woad from Picardy in northern France (the plant was pulverised and the powder used for blue dye). In 1294 the goods of all Frenchmen in England were confiscated and they had more woad at Lynn than any other port. So important had the cloth trade become by 1300 that a royal 'ulnager' or inspector was stationed in the town. The new cloth manufacturing districts of Yorkshire and the South West as well as East Anglia overshadowed the old textile towns of the East Midlands by 1500.

Yet cloth was being exported from Boston and Lynn to the Baltic in the 15th century, not least by Coventry men. The Norfolk seaport was moreover a collecting point for cloths made in Yorkshire and Suffolk for export to the Baltic in the 16th century.

Though this paper has concentrated on Lynn's major export and import trades in the Middle Ages, it should be noted that there were minor trades in a variety of merchandise, particularly about 1500. Owen refers to the import of millstones, leather goods, brass, furniture, flax, spectacles, rolls of hair, cork, onions, hats, paving tiles and purses. In 1503-04 custom accounts list furs, cloth, feather beds, lamps, copper kettles, drinking glasses, tankards, knives, scissors, market baskets, straw hats and musical instruments. Hops, sugar, fish, grindstones, bricks, tiles, carpets, tapestries, frying pans, playing cards, paper, vinegar and looking glasses were brought by Lynn merchants from Antwerp.

Boston and Lynn may have been more central to English overseas trade in the 12th and 13th centuries than in 1500, with London then making all provincial ports far more peripheral, but their commercial intercourse with Europe continued. Carus-Wilson concludes that, although these Wash ports were now outside the mainstream of England's international trade, their hinter-lands remained extensive and moderately prosperous.

4. Lynn and the German Hanse

German merchants from the Baltic and Hamburg secured trading privileges at Lynn in 1271 and these were confirmed, after serious local disputes, in 1310. The right to maintain their own houses was a critical concession (other alien merchants had to lodge with burgesses). Dollinger tells us that Lübeckers and other merchants from the East appear to be visiting English ports at the beginning of the 13th century, following traders from Gotland, to Yarmouth, Lynn, Hull and Boston, then to London.[17] Friedland has also referred to Lynn and Boston as destinations for Hanseatic merchants trying to establish themselves in the West. The town authorities accepted them as 'the fraternity of the German Hanse' (*fratres de hansa alemanies in Anglia existentes*, Lynn 1302), whereas in Sweden they were called 'the merchants from the sea towns whom one calls the Hanse brothers'.[18]

The German Hanse was able to exert a profound influence on European overseas trade by negotiating privileges and kontors or commercial head-quarters in Novgorod, Bergen, London and Brüges. Braudel sees Bruges as the crossroads of a new European economy with Hanse ships and Italian galleys nestling in its port. The German success rested on the export to the West of Baltic and Russian goods so much in demand there - timber, furs, iron, corn, wax and fish - via Lübeck, Danzig and other Hanseatic towns.

Salt, wool, cloth and wine were the main commodities they sought in distant North Sea and Atlantic havens.

Boston and Lynn attracted the German Hanse because their extensive hinterlands offered commercial opportunities and rewards. They travelled West for wool in the 13th century, thus appearing at the annual summer fairs, as did the Lübeckers at Boston in 1271. Once the export of wool from England began to fall in the middle decades of the 14th century, Hanse towns tended to link up with particular English ports. Hanseatic trade to Boston was interlocked with the kontor at Bergen where Lübeckers enjoyed a dominant role; their ships carried fish to the Wash and took away wool, cloth and salt. Lynn merchants made Danzig their chief destination from the 1380s and, sure enough, it was ships from Danzig that had already started to visit the Norfolk seaport, though Hamburg and Bremen men traded through Lynn too.[19] It seems that the Germans also imported some of their expertise in sea marking (pole beacons for example) into Lynn and Boston, whose approaches remain difficult because of the shifting sandbanks.

Herring, timber, wax, iron and pitch were imported into England via Lynn in Hanse bottoms which sometimes carried grain from the Wash to Flanders (it was exported from Prussia so the Baltic could not have been their destination). Wool, skins, cloth and lead were the commodities taken back to Danzig and other Hanse harbours. Lynn merchants sent goods to Prussia in Danzig ships as the Bittering brothers did in 1338 with a cargo of Bay salt. In 1404 several Lynn men despatched cloth to Danzig in a Dutch boat. In 1417 the *Mariknight* of Danzig was said to be owned partly by English merchants and partly by Germans whilst the master was from Bremen. In 1409 the master of the *Mariknight* had been from Danzig, and Lynn traders used it to export cloth.[20] Commercial relations between England and the Hanse broke down following the seizure of the Bay fleet by English privateers in 1449, and all the Hanseatic towns united against England after a major incident off Denmark in 1468. Trade continued up to that time with Hanse boats still arriving in Lynn in the course of 1467.

Peace between the Hanse and England was negotiated at Utrecht in 1473/74 after several years of warfare, and the German delegation seems to have achieved most of its diplomatic goals. It is most interesting to note that Lynn was on the agenda. The Germans insisted on a free gift of their former trading posts or steelyards at London and Boston and of a new one at Lynn. The Treaty of Utrecht was signed in 1474 and the English King transferred a quay and tenements in the Norfolk town to the Hanse. Lübeck invited Danzig to take charge of the property, the complex now known as St Margaret's House. The Germans had finally secured a trading post or steelyard in Lynn. Its acquisition completed a nice diplomatic victory for the Hanseatic cities whose authorities had found English merchants from the

Wash particularly troublesome. Yet the commercial aspect of this action should not be overlooked. Indeed, the Hanse diplomats at Utrecht had requested a new house and warehouse in 'the Chequer' (now King Street), where the water was deeper for their ships. Even the King had not been able to grant this!

By the 1320s some Lynn merchants were sending goods to Bergen in Lübeck ships and bringing back fish, but none of them appear to have been resident in Norway or Hanseatic cities on the Baltic until the 1380s. Cloth from England was exchanged for Baltic goods (wainscot, canvas, potash and wax). Lloyd has amply demonstrated how Lynn was more heavily dependent on the Prussia trade through Danzig than any other English port. Conflict between English and Hanseatic merchants was no doubt inevitable. In 1391 Lynn men in Stralsund had been put under house arrest for no apparent reason. English vessels in Danzig were arrested in 1396 and this damaged the interests of Lynn men more than others. Though English merchants were pushed or shunted out of the Baltic in the 1390s, and on later occasions, they persisted, not least because the Hanse had already ejected them from Bergen.[21]

Lynn and Boston traders took cloth to the Baltic in their own ships, or hired Hanse bottoms, working closely with German merchants in Danzig and elsewhere. The attention given by historians to trouble or conflict between the two nations should not obscure the long periods of peaceful co-existence and co-operation in Baltic harbours. English merchants might take their families to Hanse cities; Lynn or Boston men might marry German women. A notable example is the son of Margery Kempe. He married a Prussian woman and both travelled to Lynn in 1431, leaving their child in Danzig. Unfortunately, Margery's son died in Lynn and she escorted her daughter-in-law back to Danzig.[22] There appears also to have been an exchange or transfer of sailors and artisans between Wash and Baltic seaports. A sizeable group of German shoemakers were living in Lynn by the 1420s for example.

It is clear that a number of Lynn merchants and their associates had settled in several Baltic towns by the early years of the 15th century, particularly in Rostock, Wismar, Stralsund and Danzig as well as in Skania. That Lynn treated independently with the Hanse cities in the resolution of disputes or grievances testifies to a not inconsiderable presence. Details of this commercial and diplomatic interaction can be found in the memorandum book belonging to William Asshebourne, Lynn's town clerk. In 1408 he received a letter from Lynn men in Danzig setting out their ordinances recently drawn up for 'their company' there. Another letter arrived in the town in 1409 from the authorities in this same place relating to the grievances of 'a resident in the English nation in Danzig'.[23]

English merchants in Baltic ports demanded reciprocity or similar trading privileges to those enjoyed by the Hanse in England and this involved often protracted and painful negotiation. Royal embassies to Hanseatic cities usually included Lynn men, the recognised experts on Prussia especially. English/Hanse trading agreements were concluded in 1388, 1409 and 1437 but each was broken by further outbreaks of hostilities. Then international relations rapidly deteriorated after the attack by English privateers on the Bay fleet of Hanse and Dutch ships taking salt to the Baltic in 1449.[24]

The English turned to Iceland for new commercial opportunities as conflict with the Hanse made the penetration of the Baltic and Bergen more difficult. This North Atlantic island was, however, under the sovereignty of the King of Denmark and Lübeck men were permitted to supply its inhabitants with grain. Lynn traders took cloth and general cargo to Iceland for fish after 1412. Hanse merchants in Bergen complained to the King of Denmark who received petitions from the English too. In 1426 Lynn men in the Iceland trade were called to the Trinity Guildhall and informed that their voyages must end for the sake of international peace. The Bishop of Iceland even accused the Lynn merchants of kidnapping Icelandic children and bringing them back to the Wash. They were to resume the voyage to Iceland in the 1520s when a fleet of fourteen vessels from the Norfolk port were annually visiting this northern land.[25]

Notes

[1] Poole, A.L. *From Domesday Book to Magna Carta 1087-1216* (Oxford,1985), pp. 96, 353, 435 for references to the custom duty of 1203/04, Jewish traders and royal galleys at Lynn.

[2] Owen, D. (ed) *The Making of King's Lynn: A Documentary Survey* (Oxford, 1984), pp. 34-40 for town government and the conflicts between Bishop and Mayor with the Community of Lynn. Bishop's Lynn became King's Lynn in 1537 when the lordship of the Norwich bishops was finally ended.

[3] Darby, H.C. *The Changing Fenland* (Cambridge, 1983), p. 31.

[4] Owen, D. (ed) *The Making of King's Lynn: A Documentary Survey* (Oxford, 1984) p. 49.

[5] Braudel, F. *Civilisation and Capitalism 15th-18th Century: The Wheels of Commerce* (London, 1983), pp. 82-92.

[6] Darby, H.C. *The Changing Fenland* (Cambridge, 1983), p. 34. This is a fascinating and authoritative text for this topic.

[7] Carter, A. & Clarke, H. *Excavations in King's Lynn 1963-1970* (London, 1977), p. 445.

[8] Hoskins, W.G. *The Age of Plunder: The England of Henry VIII 1500-1547* (London, 1980), p. 194.

[9] Defoe, D. Tour Through the Eastern Counties (Ipswich, 1984 edition), pp. 115-116.

[10] Parker, V. *The Making of King's Lynn* (Chichester, 1971), p. 4. There are chapters on Lynn's medieval hinterland and its secular buildings 1100-1700.

[11] Carus-Wilson, E.M. 'The Medieval Trade of the Ports of the Wash' in *Medieval Archaeology (1962-63)*. A rich and interesting article which has proved invaluable in answering this question.

[12] Friedland, K. *Maritime Food Transport* (Köln, 1994), pp. 9-13.

13 Richards, P. *King's Lynn* (Chichester, 1990), pp. 18-31 for the hinterland and a discussion of Lynn's overseas trade 1100-1800.

14 Owen, D. (ed) *The Making of King's Lynn: A Documentary Survey* (Oxford, 1984) p. 52.

15 Harrison, R. (ed) *The Chancery Rolls: References to King's Lynn*, Vol 5, (King's Lynn, 1995), pp. 815-816. References to the wine trade and all other aspects of Lynn's medieval commerce can be found in these volumes put together by Mr Harrison. The Melchbournes mentioned in this paper feature in Vol 5.

16 Williams, N.J. *The Maritime Trade of the East Anglian Ports 1550-1590* (Oxford, 1988), p. 119. This text contains a great deal of useful information on the Port of Lynn including its role in exporting cloth to the Baltic.

17 Dollinger, P. *Die Hanse* (Stuttgart, 1989), pp. 60-61.

18 Friedland, K. *Die Hanse* (Stuttgart, 1991), p. 126.

19 Jenks, S. 'King's Lynn and the Hanseatic League in the Middle Ages', Civic Society lecture at King's Lynn (August, 1997). I owe much to the work of Dr Jenks concerning Lynn's connection with the Hanse and the setting up of the steelyard in the town in 1475. Dollinger says that the London Steelyard had a strong grip on England's other Hanseatic establishments at Ipswich, Yarmouth, Lynn, Boston, Hull and Newcastle. See *Die Hanse*, pp. 142-143.

20 Owen, D. (ed) *The Making of King's Lynn: A Documentary Survey* (Oxford, 1984), pp. 46-47 and 331-336, for commentary and documents on Lynn and the Hanse.

21 Lloyd, T.H. *England and the German Hanse 1157-1611* (Cambridge, 1991), pp. 48-49 and 91-94, for Lynn merchants in the Baltic and a full account of their activities.

22 Windeatt, B.A. (translated) *The Book of Margery Kempe* (Harmondsworth, 1985), pp. 269-279.

23 Owen, D. (ed) *William Asshebourne's Book* (Norfolk Record Society, Vol XLVIII, 1981), pp. 71 and 85.

24 Lloyd, T.H. *England and the German Hanse 1157-1611* (Cambridge, 1991), pp. 137-138 and 209-211, for more useful discussion on England and the Hanse with Lynn prominent.

25 Williams, N.J. *The Maritime Trade of the East Anglian Ports 1550-1590* (Oxford, 1988), p. 95.

The Greyfriars Tower in King's Lynn survived the dissolution of the friaries in the 1530s because it was an important seamark.

East Anglian Coasts and Harbours[1]

by

Bärbel Brodt

'Do not go too near the edge. The sea has not finished yet.'[2]

In the height of summer, in August 1272, the inner peace and smooth every-day life in Norwich, the most important and most populous town of East Anglia, and one of its major inland ports, was severely disrupted. Only a few years earlier, in December 1266, the disinherited barons had attacked the city, stormed and plundered it.[3] Now, however, the troubles arose from within the walls, and 'the most disastrous riot in the annals of the city'[4] took place. The citizens were in dispute with the monks: some broke into the Cathedral Close, attacked the Cathedral monastery, killed some of the Prior's servants, destroyed monastic buildings, and even set fire to the Cathedral.[5] A furore followed, reaching beyond even Westminster to Rome. King Henry III hurried to Norwich and the city was put under a papal interdict. Many of the offenders were hanged[6] and those more fortunate fled for their lives. Norwich's liberties were seized and not restored until 1276. The citizens were ordered to contribute three thousand marks towards repairing the damage and finally the Cathedral was reconsecrated on Advent Sunday 1278, in the presence of King Edward I.

Why should this sad affair provide an opening remark in a paper on 'East Anglian Coasts and Harbours'? Because, in order to rebuild the damaged buildings, the monks needed timber, quite a lot of it. So in 1274 the city's carpenter was paid some £14 for going to the German town of Hamburg. The timber he purchased there had originated in the Baltic, and it was then brought over to England on Hamburg ships, navigated across the North Sea by Hamburg seamen until it reached the East Anglian port of Yarmouth at the cost of £4 17 shillings and 6 pence; from there it made its way towards Norwich, only twenty-five miles away, on the readily navigable river Yare at the further cost of 6 shillings and 6 pence.[7]

This is just one of many examples which signal, emphasise and reinforce the specific elements relating to the North Sea trade. You may well ask why the carpenter was sent to Hamburg for the purchase of wood. Despite large-scale clearing even before, but especially after the Norman Conquest, the kingdom could still boast sizeable forests and woodlands.[8] However, it was a good deal easier to transport wood on water than it would have been to put it on massive carts, pulled by oxen, horses, or indeed men, and haul it to Norwich. The city was used to all kinds of goods being unloaded at her quays. Most extraordinarily, a toll list, probably thirteenth century, refers to the tolls on apes and bears being imported into Norwich: forty pence per ape, and forty-two pence per bear were the requested sums.[9]

These remarks set a scene. The history of East Anglia is as complicated as it is obscure; it is also full of stories, of invading forces, of the rise and sad decline of towns, of the fate of prosperous villages and markets with tall church towers, of terrible floods in the Fens, and of large numbers of sheep. Being concerned with its coasts and harbours, one can also demonstrate to what considerable extent the history of East Anglia was shaped and determined by its geography.

What was or what is East Anglia?[10] East Anglia was once one of the kingdoms into which Anglo-Saxon England was divided,[11] probably best defined by the boundaries of the medieval see of Norwich, which comprised the two modern counties of Norfolk and Suffolk, and the south-east corner of Cambridgeshire. With regard to the western boundary, we can be certain that in part it was marked by one of the great dykes, either the Fleam or the Devil's Dyke.

The administrative structure, though not the social and tenurial structure of East Anglia, was little changed by the Norman Conquest. Then as before, there was just one sheriff for the counties of Norfolk and Suffolk. Then as before, there was just one ecclesiastical see, from 1096 at Norwich. In what follows I shall restrict myself to the counties of Norfolk and Suffolk, with, however, a tentative venture into Lincolnshire, to say a few words about Boston, because it goes with Lynn as one of the two major ports for the wide-reaching river systems which converge on the Wash.[12] In this I have depended above all on the work of Dr Rigby.[13]

So defined, East Anglia includes a large part of England. Norfolk was the fourth largest of the English counties, covering some 2054 square miles;[14] Suffolk more than half that size.[15] Two of its geographical characteristics are salient for our purposes. One is its enormously long curving coastline, the other is the conformation of the navigable rivers.[16] One group from West Norfolk and indeed West Suffolk flow northwards to the Wash where they converge with others from much of the English Midlands. A second group from South-East Norfolk and North-East Suffolk converge on Breydon Water. The third are a series of approximately parallel rivers which flow eastwards into the North Sea with estuaries along the Suffolk coast. It is these river patterns which have, above all, determined the location and nature of our ports.

These rivers served an outstandingly populous and rich area. The Domesday survey of 1086 shows that Norfolk was the most populous county in England, Suffolk the third most populous, both including areas of altogether unusual population density.[17] Even the Black Death and its

23

sequels hardly reduced the relative importance of East Anglian population.[18] Marc Bloch said, 'Let the figures speak. They have a brutal eloquence'. Another piece of brutal eloquence is the tax assessment of 1334.[19] In this Lay Subsidy, of the ten most highly assessed provincial towns, four were among those under our consideration: Norwich, once the major port of East Anglia, and still a port, Yarmouth, Lynn and Boston.

East Anglia is largely surrounded by and open to the influences of the sea. In considering my theme of the East Anglian ports, it is important to notice that good, natural harbours are far more uncommon on the East Anglian coast than a quick glance at an eighteenth century French chart would suggest.[20] It gives not only the sea-distances which enable us to comprehend how important the Narrows of the North Sea are, but by also giving us the make-up of the sea-bed, it reminds us that North Sea navigation was, not only in the Middle Ages but also for fishermen quite recently, conducted as much or more by knowledge of the sea-bed as by use of the marine compass.

A great deal of the coast is very exposed, and is surrounded by very shallow water. That is why there is no major port between Yarmouth and Lynn. Here, one should at least mention in passing the significance, albeit limited, of very small ports along the coast, like Cromer. It is, however, very difficult to estimate the volume of their medieval trade because the figures are subsumed in the accounts of the coastal head-ports. Furthermore, even where river estuaries provide promising harbours, these have through the centuries often been threatened by erosion, or by silting. Thus Yarmouth had a constant struggle to keep its harbour open; Dunwich was eroded almost entirely into the sea by the end of the Middle Ages and the fact that Orford is now so strangely a lost place is due to the silting of its harbour.

Space does not permit me to deal with the early Dark Age maritime history of East Anglia. I might, however, mention in passing that a kind of symbolic reminder of the importance of the sea in the earliest days of East Anglia is that the famous burial of c.630 at Sutton Hoo is in a ship something over ninety feet long, considerably longer than the famous Viking ships from Gokstad and Oseberg.[21] When we come to consider the ports in the Anglo-Saxon and the Anglo-Norman period, a very important thing to understand is that for a long period the most significant port was Norwich. Compare the significance of Lincoln and of York further north. The rise of major ports on the coast itself appears largely to belong to the eleventh and later centuries: Boston, Lynn, Yarmouth, Orford.

Before looking at the major ports one by one, let me stress two characteristic features of the English medieval port towns: their position within the centralised nation-wide royal customs system and local efforts to maintain the harbours and make a decent profit.

24

East Anglia showing Lynn's extensive hinterland before the coming of the railways.

The Crown had a tremendous interest in the administration of the ports along the coasts of the realm. In 1275 the national customs system was regularised on a grand scale. In order to facilitate the collection of royal customs which were due on imports and exports, the Crown divided up the coastline into some thirteen customs jurisdictions, each managed from a specifically designed head port.[22] The so-called staple system was super-imposed on the royal customs system. Originating in the thirteenth century and designed to facilitate revenue collection for the Crown, the staple system sought to channel foreign merchants to designated home staples in England, and English exports to a compulsory staple port abroad.[23] Each of the customs head ports usually had two customs collectors,[24] drawn from amongst the town's chief officers, often the mayor or the bailiffs.[25]

Port towns met the expenses which were associated with destructive acts of nature and also human hand through royal, corporate, and often individual funding efforts. Because of continual silting, for example, Great

Yarmouth had to construct no less than four new harbour entrances between 1300 and 1410.[26] In 1392, the town levied a one shilling tax on every last of herring, and received an allowance of £500 over five years out of the port's royal customs to help meet the estimated £1000 cost of the entrance it had to build in 1409. We have to bear in mind that these royal acts of favour – be it making murage grants, granting relief from taxation, or reduction of the town's fee-farm - nevertheless meant that in the long run the bulk of the expenses for the upkeep of the harbours had to be met through local taxation and often individual investment. And there was something else: the English kings had little or no permanent navy. Thus they depended almost wholly on port towns to furnish mercantile vessels and indeed a large part of their crews in order to transport troops and supplies, to control the coast and to engage the ever present enemy at sea. Thus, in the earlier fourteenth century, the North Sea fleets in the service of the English Crown came very largely from Great Yarmouth.[27] In the early stages of the Hundred Years' War, Yarmouth frequently supplied thirty to forty ships for naval service from its fleet, which probably included more than one hundred ships of over one hundred tons. After 1360, there was a great decline, to which I shall refer later.[28]

I am now going to discuss the East Anglian ports in the later Middle Ages, at a time when relations with the Hanse were important, briefly sketching highlights of their history, offering a few generalisations and concluding by seeking the help of this company to assess the role of the Hanse.[29]

Three generalisations may safely be made. First, the background to the development of the East Anglian ports is that the fortunes of those actually on the coast rose compared to those further inland. Second, during the later Middle Ages, there were extraordinarily marked ebbs and flows in the fortune of particular ports. Third, from about 1200 there was a general increase in the political freedoms secured by port towns; the economic effects of these must have been real, but are singularly hard to quantify.

My first example is Boston.[30] Apparently unimportant at the time of Domesday Book, Boston had become very important by the early 13th century at the latest. Lying only four miles from the mouth of the river Witham, it displaced Lincoln much further upstream as the principal port for a wide area. By the early thirteenth century it had become the site of a major international fair. Its great wealth at this stage can be seen by its paying £780 to the tax of a fifteenth levied between 1203 and 1205.[31] Only London paid more. This probably marked something like the peak of Boston's prosperity. In the fourteenth century it was hit by the decline of its great fair. Nevertheless, in the 1334 assessment it still appears as a very rich and important place.[32] It was a staple port for wool in 1369,[33] and as my colleagues will tell you, it was a major place of resort for the Hanse. The withdrawal of the Hanse in the late fifteenth century was a major blow. By 1565, Boston had only eight ships of its own, and most of its trade was in the hands of Lynn merchants.[34]

Where Boston is somewhat unusual among significant English towns is that in the medieval period it was not in the ordinary sense a royal borough. By a rather unusual charter in 1204 King John granted the bailiff of Boston sole jurisdiction in the town.[35] Not until the time of Henry VIII, in 1545, did it gain a royal charter, granting or confirming its rights to markets and fairs, allowing its burgesses freedom of toll throughout the kingdom and specifying other economic regulations. Commonly the grant of a royal charter was indicative of a town's success; in 1546 at Boston it looks more like an effort to reverse decline.[36]

Let us now move on along the Wash towards this, our host town, Lynn. In view of what we have already seen and heard of it, and what is bound to follow in the course of this conference, I can be fairly brief here. Lynn does not appear as of special importance in Domesday, except to the extent that it lay in a major area of salt production.[37] Its economic importance first appears in the successful effort by Herbert de Losinga, first bishop of Norwich, to establish a foothold there in the 1090s.[38] He founded a priory, subordinate to his cathedral church at Norwich, and the church of St. Margaret. It appears that there was already a significant merchant settlement at Lynn. Here, as at Boston, we have the growth, very near the coast, of a port where there had been no coastal port before.

As at Boston we can see that there had been major development by the beginning of the 13th century. Lynn paid £600 to the tax of 1203-05.[39]By this time it seems to have had a laid-out grid pattern of streets and, not one market place, but two (a rare feature, paralleled at Beccles in Suffolk), and additionally another major church, dedicated (characteristically of a sea-port) to St Nicholas.

Lynn's constitutional history is rather special. It began, or largely began, as a seigniorial borough. Its name was Bishop's Lynn, not King's Lynn, until the 16th century. However, in 1204, a series of charters from king and bishop established Lynn with a set of liberties and privileges, corresponding to those of a free royal town.[40] I have investigated the complicated mechanisms of the internal government at Lynn elsewhere.[41] Its mercantile community had an inner life and a status which must have mattered to them. An indication of the difference between its status and that of Boston was that from 1283 Lynn was represented in Parliament,[42] whereas Boston was not. In considering the trade of Lynn, about which you will hear more from others, I should like briefly to mention an element which, considered from the Hanseatic point of view, one might overlook: the importance of internal coasting trade of a kind which generally does not appear in the Customs Accounts.[43] Thus, in the later 16th century, Lynn depended considerably on trade with north-eastern England, receiving about 20,000 tons of coal[44] annually from Newcastle, and in return sending grain. There were probably corresponding trades earlier.

Moving south-eastwards from Lynn we have no major port until we come to Yarmouth.[45] Here I should emphasise that both on the Norfolk coast and on that of Suffolk, there were small ports which sometimes reached a certain importance, and which cannot be investigated through the Customs Accounts.

Yarmouth[46] fits approximate into the pattern of other East Anglian ports. Lying as it did at the point of convergence of a river system which served a very populous area, it was a nodal point of special significance. By the 14th century parts of this area could almost be described as industrialised. The centre of a major textile industry was located there which took its name from an unchartered industrial village called Worstead. (I should mention in passing that that invaluable work, Carus-Wilson and Coleman, *England's Export Trade*, is not so helpful on the subject of worsted as might be hoped: it has a broadcloth bias.) Yarmouth was at the time of Domesday a relatively unimportant but rising place. Just as Lynn lies near a confluence of rivers which drain eight counties, so does Yarmouth control a major confluence, that of the rivers Yare, Ant, Bure, Thurne and Waveney. Of crucial importance was the link along the Yare, such that Yarmouth almost controlled Norwich's access to the sea. We can well assume that even before Yarmouth obtained its first charter in 1208, it had already deprived Norwich of most of its maritime trade. During the next two centuries, the Norwich officials complained repeatedly of Yarmouth preventing ships and merchants coming up the Yare and indeed preventing Norwich's merchants trading at Yarmouth.[47] But the two towns were mutually dependent. It has been convincingly pointed out that 'inconvenient and distasteful though the existence of Yarmouth was to Norwich, the two towns were complementary. ... They should be regarded almost as together constituting one town'.[48]

Great Yarmouth also resembles Lynn in that here too Herbert de Losinga tried to establish his authority, though with less success. Another resemblance is the provision of a fine parish church, again dedicated to St Nicholas, and by the end of the Middle Ages argued to be the largest in England. Yarmouth has for the student of urban topography a special interest. It lies on a long and narrow peninsula of sand,[49] between the North Sea and Breydon Water which is formed by the rivers Yare, Waveney and Bure. Its immensely crowded site produced a town-plan whereby its principal features were no less than 145 exceedingly narrow lanes, so called rows, a few feet wide, running from east to west. One could have no more remarkable a demonstration of how urban topography conformed to the need to pack population and wealth into a narrow site.

Yarmouth's constitutional history falls into a common pattern. Again a charter from King John was crucial. In 1208 he gave the burgesses of Yarmouth general liberties according to the customs of Oxford (as had been the case with Lynn), a gild merchant and weekly courts.[50] This charter was amplified by several later charters asserting the rights of the borough[51] against neighbouring Little Yarmouth and Gorleston, situated further south.

Yarmouth, like Lynn, was subject to ebbs and flows of importance. In the tax of 1203-05 it paid £90,[52] a decent sum, but far below those paid by Lynn and Boston. The contrast becomes stronger in the later Middle Ages. Lynn's population dropped catastrophically from an estimated near 6,000 in 1377 to less than 1,500 in 1524. Yarmouth's remained much more stable at over 3,000 through the same period.[53]

But Yarmouth had fluctuating and, in the later Middle Ages, declining fortunes. In the fourteenth century Great Yarmouth was prosperous and drew most of its wealth from shipping and fishing. It was the autumn herring fair, only outstripped by that at Scania, which put the name Great Yarmouth firmly on the merchants' maps. The fair which took place between Michaelmas and Martinmas, had originally been regulated by barons of the Cinque Ports, and many a quarrel arose over its jurisdiction and privileges until Great Yarmouth secured the royal privileges which left the town in charge of the fair.[54] Visitors came from places in Scandinavia, in Italy and Spain. As we can gather from Yarmouth's murage accounts of around 1340, each year about five hundred ships and as many as seven hundred individuals from some fifty continental and over one hundred English settlements paid murage. About three-quarters of the visitors and about half of the ships were charged for herring. And yet, these accounts barely reflect the true size of either the Yarmouth or the English fishing fleet. In 1329 the French were hoping to destroy one thousand English fishing boats at Great Yarmouth.[55] These prosperous times were not to last. The population of the town was probably reduced by a third by the Black Death of 1348-1349. But this alone will not explain Yarmouth's misfortune. The decline of its chief industries, the heavy cost of two major public works, namely the town's walls and the town's harbour, and finally the almost constant burdens of war against Scotland and France, all contributed to ensure that for the remainder of the Middle Ages Yarmouth fared much worse than almost all other English towns. In terms of tax ranking, for example, only Shrewsbury and Winchester among the twenty leading towns of the 1334 Lay Subsidy had fallen further than Yarmouth by the 1520s.[56] The problem facing Yarmouth's herring industry was not principally one of rising costs and falling demands, but rather of reduced landings. Here is another striking example of the close relationship between geography and constitutional history. Having shaken off the juridical threat of the barons of the Cinque Ports, the Yarmouth municipal officers now found themselves in competition with neighbouring Lowestoft over a sheltered stretch of coastal water named Kirkley Roads:[57]this was outside Yarmouth's jurisdiction, no toll had to be paid there, no Yarmouth customs could be collected.[58] Even when Yarmouth finally succeeded in preventing the diversion of the herring trade to Lowestoft, the victory was a rather empty one. The entire East Anglian herring fishery was by now threatened by the Low Countries. Their industry expanded as the East Anglian one declined, because of its greater emphasis on quality, its use of larger vessels and salting at sea, and its development of improved curing techniques.

Poor Yarmouth, but wait until I tell you about our next port on the journey south: Dunwich.[59] At the time of Domesday, Dunwich was clearly a flourishing port worth £50 a year and paying 60,000 herrings annually to the king.[60] It fits into the pattern of the rising ports actually on the coast. Until the 14th century it had all the characteristics of a successful East Anglian port town. It had received, like others, a charter of King John,[61] making it *liber burgus*. It is recorded in the reign of Edward I as possessing some 36 ships and barks, trading to the North Sea, Iceland and elsewhere, with 24 fishing-boats and maintaining 11 ships of war.[62] Dunwich had six churches by 1254. But from the late 13th century it was subject to tremendous erosion from the sea. By 1347 over 400 houses had been destroyed and a number of churches.[63] This once prosperous town was completely eroded away; it retained a kind of life into the 16th century, but by the 18th there was, as now, nothing but a scattered village and a few remains on the edge of a cliff. 'Be careful, if you look at it. Do not go too near the edge. The sea has not finished yet'.[64]

As we move down the coast from Yarmouth to Ipswich we have, however unwilling as historians, to take even more account of geography. This coastline has a very special geography, carefully studied by the late Ernest Clifford Steer. For reasons too deep, or as it turned out, often too shallow for historians to go into, there is a recurrent pattern of long estuaries, developing parallel to the coasts, and endlessly silting up. The case of Yarmouth is paradigm. If I had time I could show you a similar evolution on a less important, but still significant scale, in the minor ports of Southwold and Aldeburgh. In the 15th century both had a more than local significance as bases for the Iceland fishery for knowledge of which we owe so much to the late Professor Carus-Wilson.

It is with this in mind that I move to Orford.[65] Orford, which was shown on a map drawn by John Norden in 1601,[66] is now a very strange place.

The purpose of this map is also to illustrate a marked feature of the coast all the way from Yarmouth to the Essex border: the creation of long estuaries parallel to the coast, and prone to silting. The extreme cases are the Yare estuary at Yarmouth and that of the Alde and Ore going past this town of Orford. It is a spread-out village with the characteristics of a lost town. It is near a sea which is almost impossible to reach. It is situated on a long, shallow estuary. In the twelfth century, it was a key point[67] on the coast. That is why Henry II in the 1160s built a brand new castle there on the most modern plan. This castle was accompanied by what seems to have been a newly laid out town. We have here a somewhat late example of the new town on the coast.[68] Orford conforms in general terms to the usual pattern. It gained a charter as *liber burgus* in 1256,[69] confirmed with additions in 1326. Assessed at the urban rate in 1334 it does not stand out as more than a place of middling importance: £10, a tenth of the Yarmouth assessment.[70] Orford was beyond doubt a successful urban foundation, but it started to decline towards the end of the Middle Ages, due to constant silting, and for today's visitor it feels a strangely lost town, tucked away behind the length of Orford Ness.

Finally, Ipswich.[71] Ipswich is in a sense the most mysterious and certainly the least studied of our towns, apart from the work of Geoffrey Martin. Let us have a quick look at something which I have referred to before, and which may not be completely familiar to our German colleagues. That is to say the standard English statistics, with all faults acknowledged. In Domesday Book, Ipswich appears as follows. There had been 538 burgesses in 1066, but their number had dropped to 220 in 1086.[72] Despite this, the town's value had risen to £37, thus placing Ipswich in terms of the value put on it at 18th among the provincial towns. In 1334 it was assessed in the urban tenth at £64. In 1377 it had 1507 taxpayers and ranked in those terms 26th. Ipswich is the only one amongst those towns I have presented today which fails to fit neatly into my scheme. One might be tempted to suggest that Orford is to Ipswich what Yarmouth is to Norwich, or, indeed, Boston to Lincoln. As with so many good ideas, it does not really work. Ipswich is the one place of those I have been discussing, which has an archaeologically studied and significant past in the Dark Ages. I leave Ipswich, though the merchants of Cologne did not, in the admission of ignorance.

I had originally intended to use this opportunity to speak about the Hanseatic merchants in the East Anglian towns, but as I am in the company of those far better qualified to do so than myself, I have decided against this. A few very general comments will suffice before, in conclusion, I return to the East Anglian landscape in which they lived, moved and traded.

There is a long standing agreement amongst historians on either side of the Channel that the merchants of the German Hanse, who came to control the bulk of the Baltic trade in raw materials to England, were the most influential foreign traders in her eastern ports. It was especially at London, Hull, Boston, Lynn, Sandwich and Ipswich that the Hansards captured a significant portion of trade. Largely priced out of the wool trade due to the differential customs rates on alien wool exports, their other trading privileges in England, including most significantly a lower customs rate on cloth exports, were the main reasons for this. Until the end of the fourteenth century Boston has to be considered the leading provincial centre of the Hanseatic trade. At Lynn the volume of Hanseatic trade was smaller, but crucial in terms of Lynn's overall trade since almost one-third of it was in the hands of Hanse merchants.

The London *Kontor* was very much the centre of the Hanse community in England well before the end of the twelfth century, but it was not until the end of the fourteenth century that the *Stalhof* acquired what amounted to a virtual monopoly of trade. The composition of the *Stalhof* was quite international, while that of the provincial trading posts had a distinctly regional bias: Lübeck at Boston, the Prussians at Hull, Danzig and Bremen merchants in Lynn, the Hamburg merchants at Great Yarmouth and the merchants of Cologne in Ipswich.[73]

No one considering the other contributors and contributions to this Colloquium will be surprised that my reference to the Hanse is so brief. The very existence of the present gathering is sufficient indication of the extent to which North Sea studies have been focused on and indebted to the study of the Hanse. Seen from the perspective of East Anglia and the long, sometimes well-documented, sometimes barely known history of its ports, the Hanse, even in the days of its glory, cannot be seen as more than one major force and factor among many. The story or stories I have tried to tell are fragments of a large, complicated, and important piece of history, in which the Hanse has a key part. There is something on which we all might agree, that the subjects of our common concern can be fully understood only in the context of the North Sea world (not to speak of wider circles) as a whole. Let me just repeat considerations, bearing on the history of Great Yarmouth. What were the reasons which determined the appearance, and fairly soon the dominance, on the English North Sea coast of ports actually on the seashore, like Yarmouth, rather than at nodal river points inland, like Norwich? Were these causes specifically English, or did they relate to factors having more to do with developments in the nature of shipping? How far was the exploitation and the movement of the immense shoals of spawning herring a formative factor in North Sea economies? How far was war an economic determinant? For example, could it be that the virtual disappearance of the major Yarmouth merchant fleet was due to the demands of the English Crown, leaving less burdened ship-owners on other coasts to take the advantage? We can all, no doubt we all do, ask such questions; the answers, I imagine you would agree, can only be found through collective endeavour to produce what one might call, in short hand, a Braudel for the North Sea.

Notes

[1] Revised version of a paper given at Hansisches Kolloquium King's Lynn, 4-7.6.1998. I wish to thank the organisers of the Colloquium for inviting me, and the participants for their helpful comments in the discussion. I am especially grateful to James Campbell for sharing his vast knowledge of East Anglia with me and placing his extensive library at my disposal.

[2] Rowland Parker, *Men of Dunwich. The Story of a Vanished Town*, London, 1978, p.264.

[3] Their plunder was said to have been worth twenty thousand marks and to have filled one hundred and forty carts. See James Campbell, 'Norwich', in: Mary D. Lobel & E. Henry Johns (eds.), *The Atlas of Historic Towns*, vol.ii, London / Oxford, 1975, p.9.

[4] William Hudson & John Cottingham Tingey (eds.), *The Records of the City of Norwich*, ii vols, Norwich 1906 / 1910, here vol .i, p.xxx.

[5] See Bartholomæus de Cotton, *Historia Anglicana; (A.D. 449-1298) Necnon Ejusdem Liber de Archiepiscopis et Episcopis Angliae*, ed. by Henry Richards Luard (Rolls Series 16), 1859, pp. 146-154; Thomas Stapleton (ed.), *Liber de Antiquis Legibus* (Camden Society, old series, 34), 1846, pp. 145-148; Walter Rye, 'The Riot between the Monks and Citizens of Norwich in 1272', in: *Norfolk Antiquarian Miscellany*, 2 (1883), pp. 17-89.

[6] See *Chronica Buriensis 1212-1301. The Chronicle of Bury St. Edmunds 1212-1301*, ed. Antonia Gransden, London 1964, pp. 50-52, here p. 52 on punishment of offenders.

[7] Campbell, Norwich, p. 14, n. 94; Herbert Washington Saunders, *An Introduction to the Obedientiary & Manor Rolls of Norwich Cathedral Priory*, Norwich, 1930, pp. 87-88.

[8] See Henry Clifford Darby, *Domesday England*, Cambridge, 1977, esp. pp. 171-207.

[9] Hudson & Tingey, *Records*, vol. ii, p. 202. This list of tolls is undated, but there is reason to believe that this document was drawn up in the thirteenth century as part of the city's Book of Customs.

[10] See also Bärbel Brodt, 'East Anglia' in: David M. Palliser (ed.), *The Cambridge Urban History of Britain, vol. i*, Chapter 22d, Cambridge, forthcoming 1998.

[11] 'East Anglia', in: *The Encyclopedia Britannica*. Eleventh Edition, published in twenty-nine volumes, New York 1910-1911, vol. viii, pp. 827-828, passim. This entry is primarily based upon Bede's *Historia Ecclesiastica Gentis Anglorum*, and there Bede gives no information about its origin, except that its earliest settlers were Angles.

[12] See Eleanora Carus-Wilson, 'The Medieval Trade of the Ports of the Wash' in: *Medieval Archaeology vi (1962)*, pp. 182-201.

[13] Stephen H. Rigby, *Boston and Grimsby in the Middle Ages*, Phil. Diss. (masch.), London, 1983; Stephen H. Rigby, *Medieval Grimsby: Growth and Decline*, Hull, 1993; Stephen H. Rigby, 'Sore Decay and Fair Dwellings: Boston and Urban Decline in the Later Middle Ages', in: *Midland History 10* (1985), pp. 47-61. See also Michael Jonathan Taunton Lewis & Neil Richard Wright, *Boston as a Port*, Lincoln, 1973 (=Lincolnshire Industrial Archaeological Special Issue, viii).

[14] David Dymond, *The Norfolk Landscape*, London, 1985 (=The Making of the English Landscape 19), p. 23, and map on pp. 154-155. See also Bärbel Brodt, *Städte ohne Mauern. Stadtentwicklung im 14.Jahrhundert in East Anglia*, Paderborn, 1997 (=Veröffentlichungen des Deutschen Historischen Instituts London, Bd. 44, esp. Chapter ii, pp. 17-31.

[15] Norman Scarfe, *The Suffolk Landscape*, 2nd. ed. London, 1975 (=The Making of the English Landscape 6), p. 27, and map on p. 166.

[16] John C. Barringer, 'The Rivers of Norfolk and North Suffolk', in Lewis M. Munby (ed.), *East Anglian Studies*, Cambridge, 1968, pp. 1-17.

[17] Henry Clifford Darby, 'The Domesday Geography of Norfolk and Suffolk', in: *Geographical Journal 85* (1935), pp. 432-452.

[18] Leslie Gordon Cole, 'The Black Death in East Anglia', in: *East Anglian Magazine 18* (1959), pp. 554-558.

[19] See below with reference to Boston and the other East Anglian ports.

[20] The original of the chart is owned by James Campbell. It is called 'The North Sea with the Kattegat'. From the Chart of Messrs de Verdun, de Borda, and Pingré, made public in MDCCLXXVII, by Order of Louis XVI; constructed on a larger scale and with considerable Additions and Emendations, by L.S. de la Rochette, London MDCCXCVI.

[21] The remains of which are both on display at the University Museum of National Antiquities at Oslo, Norway. See James Campbell et al. (eds.), *The Anglo-Saxons*, London, 1982, esp. pp. 148-150, plates 140, 141; for Sutton Hoo see there pp. 32-34.

[22] In the early fifteenth century, the number of head ports rose to fifteen: Bridgewater, carved out of the Bristol jurisdiction, and Plymouth/Fowey, separated out of the Exeter customs jurisdiction, were added. See Maryanne Kowaleski, 'Port Towns', in: Palliser (ed.), *Cambridge Urban History*, chapter 19, passim.

[23] For the boundaries of the customs jurisdictions and the changes they underwent, see Eleanora Carus-Wilson & Olive Coleman, *England's Export Trade 1275-1540*, Oxford, 1963, pp. 175-193. For an overview of the staple system see Ephraim Lipson, *The Economic History of England*, vol. i, London, 1959, pp. 550.567.

[24] N.J. Williams, *The Maritime Trade of the East Anglian Ports*, Phil. Diss. (masch.), Oxford, 1952, esp. Introduction, pp. 1-10, demonstrates, however, that during the sixteenth century the coastal administration in East Anglia - unlike London - was remarkably ineffective, its officers were quite incapable of controlling all shipments along the lengthy coastline.

[25] See Raymond William King Hinton (ed.), *The Port Books of Boston 1601-1640*, Hereford, 1956 (=The Publications of the Lincoln Record Society, 50), p. xiii-xviii.

[26] Kowaleski, Port Towns; Anthony Saul, *Great Yarmouth in the Fourteenth Century. A Study in Trade, Politics and Society*, Phil. Diss. (Masch.), Oxford, 1975, here pp. 38-39.

[27] Anthony Saul, 'English Towns in the Later Middle Ages: The Case of Great Yarmouth', in: *Journal of Medieval History* 8, (1982), pp. 75-88, here p. 77; Saul, *Great Yarmouth*, p. 123.

[28] Saul, 'English Towns', pp. 79-80, 85.

[29] For the sixteenth century see Williams, *The Maritime Trade*.

[30] Pishey Thompson, *History and Antiquities of Boston and the Hundred of Skirbeck*, Boston, 1856. There are very few records which can shed light on the municipal development of Boston. See Lincolnshire Archives Office, *The Records of the Borough of Boston*, Lincoln, 1964; most recently: Jennifer & Peter Clark (eds.), *The Boston Assembly Minutes 1545-1575*, Woodbridge, 1987 (=Publications of the Lincoln Record Society, 77).

[31] Norman Scott Brien Gras, *The Early English Customs System. A documentary Study of the Institutional and Economic History of the Customs from the Thirteenth to the Sixteenth Century*, (=Harvard Economic Studies, vol.xviii), Cambridge/Mass., 1918, pp.221-222, p.222 for Boston figure.

[32] £73 6 shillings 8 pence. Compare this to the three taxation boroughs in that county: Lincoln was taxed at a tenth with £100, Stamford with £35, and finally Grimsby with a mere £9. Rigby, 'Sore Decay', p. 54, n.54 (=P.R.O. E179/135/19). See also Robin E. Glasscock (ed.), *The Lay Subsidy of 1334* (=Records of Social and Economic History, New Series 11), London, 1975, pp. 167-186 for Lincolnshire assessment; p. 187 for taxation sums of Lincoln, and Grimsby, p. 169 for Boston and Stamford.

[33] Thompson, *History and Antiquities*, p. 55.

[34] See Clark & Clark, *Assembly Minutes*, p. xi. The documents relating to the survey can be found in Historical Manuscripts Commission, Salisbury MSS., II, 315. On state of harbour and four quays see also Hinton, *Port Books*, here p. xi.

[35] Thompson, *History and Antiquities*, p. 38, no. 2. Maurice Warwick Beresford & Herbert Patrick Reginald Finberg, *English Medieval Boroughs - A Hand-List*, Newton Abbot, 1973, p. 136, wrongly give the date 1285, referring to Thompson, p. 43. There Thompson, however, is concerned with a murage-grant by King Edward I in 1285, listing the individual tolls and customs on goods coming into the city.

[36] Martin Weinbaum (ed.), *British Borough Charters 1307-1660*, Cambridge, 1943, pp. 69-70 (=Letters and Papers Henry VIII, xx. pt. 1 g. 846 (38).

[37] The relevant entry in Domesday Book records some 180 active salterns close to Lynn.

[38] Carus-Wilson, 'Medieval Trade', p.182; Vanessa Parker, *The Making of King's Lynn. Secular Buildings from the 11th to the 17th century*, London/Chichester, 1971, esp. pp. 1-8; Brodt, *Städte ohne Mauern*, esp. pp. 148-152.

[39] Gras, *English Customs*, p. 222.

[40] Four years later, in 1208, Great Yarmouth became the second East Anglian borough to receive the liberties of Oxford. In the case of Lynn, oddly enough, the first of three charters in that year was issued by King John at Lambeth on 17 January 1204. This was followed by one of the bishop on 24 March 1204, again to be confirmed by the king on 4 September. It is most striking, however, that none of the three charters mention the fee-farm.

[41] Brodt, *Städte ohne Mauern*, esp. pp. 234-265.

[42] Francis Palgrave (ed.), *The Parliamentary Writs and Writs of Military Summons, together with the Records and Muniments relating to ... the King's High Court of Parliament and the Councils of the Realm*, ii vols, London, 1827/1834, vol. i, p.lxix; vol. ii. pp. ccxxiv-ccixxv.

[43] In the medieval period - as opposed to the 16th and 17th centuries - customs records relating to trade between one part of England and another are by no means common. The best sources are those for local tolls, for which see H.S. Cobb, 'Local Port Customs Prior to 1550', in *Journal of the Society of Archivists*, i, no. 8, 1958.

[44] Williams, *Maritime Trade*, p. vii.

[45] There is no better account of Yarmouth for the period with which we are concerned than Saul, *Great Yarmouth*; see also Saul, 'English Towns'.

[46] Henry Harrod, *Repertory of Deeds and Documents relating to the Borough of Great Yarmouth*, Great Yarmouth, 1855; Henry Manship, *A Booke of the Foundacion and Antiquitye of the Towne of Great Yarmouthe; from the original Manuscripts written in the time of Queen Elizabeth; with Notes and an Appendix*, ed. by Charles John Palmer, Great Yarmouth, 1847; Charles John Palmer, *The History of Great Yarmouth, designed as a Continuation of Manship's History of that Town*, Great Yarmouth/London, 1856; Charles John Palmer, *The Perlustration of Great Yarmouth, with Gorleston and Southtown*, iii vols., Great Yarmouth, 1872-1875; Henry Swinden, *The History and Antiquities of the ancient Burgh of Great Yarmouth, in the County of Norfolk. Collected from the Corporation Charters, Records and Evidences, and other most authentic Materials*, Norwich, 1772.

[47] For example, see Hudson & Tingey, *Records*, vol. i, pp. 62-64 (=Book of Pleas, fol.xxi), or vol. ii, pp. 197-199 (=Book of Customs, fol.2).

[48] Campbell, Norwich, p. 14.

[49] The title is rather telling: Arthur William & John Lewis Ecclestone, *The Rise of Great Yarmouth: the Story of a Sandbank*, Great Yarmouth, 1959.

[50] *Rotuli Chartarum*, p. 175.

[51] In its medieval hey-day the borough's fortifications included an area of around 130 hectares. See Charles John Palmer, 'The Town Wall of Great Yarmouth', in *Norfolk Archaeology* 6 (1864), pp. 106-124, here p. 106.

[52] Gras, *English Customs*, p. 222.

[53] Fenwick, *Poll Taxes*, p. 230; p. 503.

[54] Saul, 'English Towns', p. 77; Calendar of Patent Rolls 1272-1281, pp. 203-204 (=1277, 8 May, Westminster); Calendar of Patent Rolls 1301-1307, p. 329 (=1305, 31 March, Westminster); Calendar of Close Rolls 1313-1318, p. 95 (=1314, 1 April, St. Albans); Calendar of Close Rolls 1354-1360, p. 357 (=1357, 3 May, Westminster).

[55] See Saul, *Great Yarmouth*, p. 191; C. de la Roncière, *L'histoire de la marine française*, Paris, 1899, here vol. i, pp. 434-435.

[56] See William George Hoskins, *Local History in England*, 2nd ed. London, 1972, pp. 238-239.

[57] Beginning approximately nine miles south of Yarmouth and stretching beyond Lowestoft. The silting of the river Yare meant that by the 1370s the entrance to Yarmouth's harbour was at Kirkley Roads.

[58] The unchartered town of Lowestoft disputed Yarmouth's right to collect tolls in the Roads and tried to divert trade to its own harbour. Control of the Roads was hotly disputed; it was only in 1386 that Yarmouth finally annexed the Roads. See Saul, *Great Yarmouth*, pp. 162-170; Saul, 'English Towns', esp. p. 78, n. 4.

[59] Thomas Gardner, *An historical Account of Dunwich, antiently a City, now a Borough; Blithburgh, formmerly a Town of Note, now a Village; Southwold, once a Village, now a Town Corporate*, London, 1754; N.S. Day, *Glorious Dunwich. Its Story through the Ages*, Ipswich, 1947; Parker, *Men of Dunwich*.

[60] Note the increase in value from £10 in 1066 to £50 in 1086. See *Domesday Book, Text and Translation*, ed. by John Morris, vols. 34 i + ii, Suffolk, ed. by Alex Rumble, Chichester, 1986, vol. ii, fol. 311b, 312, 331b, 333b, 385. See Brodt, *Städte ohne Mauern*, p. 328, also p. 87, 91. At the time of Domesday the town might have covered an area of some 120 Hektar. See Parker, *Men of Dunwich*, p. 142; Gardner, *Account*, p. 3; Scarfe, *Suffolk Landscape*, p. 207.

[61] See *Rotuli Chartarum*, vol. i, p. 51. The fee-farm amounted to £66.

[62] 'Dunwich' in *Encyclopedia Britannica*, p. 685.

[63] There had been six according to the 1254 valuation. See Brodt, *Städte ohne Mauern*, p. 330; William Edward Lunt (ed.), *The Valuation of Norwich*, Oxford, 1926, p. 444, 448.

[64] Parker, *Men of Dunwich*, p. 264.

[65] Scarfe, *Suffolk Landscape*, p. 126.

[66] *Orford Ness. A Selection of Maps mainly by John Norden, presented to James Alfred Steers*, Cambridge, 1966, p. 7. It is on a scale of 1 inch to the mile.

[67] Maurice Warwick Beresford, *New Towns of the Middle Ages. Town Plantation in England, Wales and Gasconny*, London, 1967, p. 489.

[68] See Vincent Burrough Redstone, 'Orford and its Castle', in *Proceedings of the Suffolk Institute for Archaeology 10* (1898-1900), pp. 205-230; R.A. Roberts, 'Orford Castle', in: *Journal of the British Archaeological Association*, New Series 34 (1928-1929), pp. 82-86.

[69] Patent Roll, 26 Edw.III, part i, membr. 29: Ipswich Record Office, HD 64/1/30; *Calendar of Charter Rolls*, vol. iii, p. 482.

[70] Willard, *Taxation Boroughs*, pp. 433-434; Glasscock, *Lay Subsidy*, p. 294.

[71] Geoffrey H. Martin, *The Borough and Merchant Community of Ipswich*, Phil.Diss. (masch.), Oxford, 1956; Lillian J. Redstone, *Ipswich through the Ages*, Ipswich, 1948.

[72] *Domesday Book, Suffolk*, vol. ii, fol. 290, 294b, 421b.

[73] Terence Henry Lloyd, *England and the German Hanse. 1157-1611: A Study of their Trade and Commercial Diplomacy*, Cambridge, 1991, p. 368. Lloyd's book is fairly useful, but there are many faults and problems as well. For example, he consistently misspells the German for 'Steelyard'.

Late Medieval Harbours:
Function and Construction

by

Detlev Ellmers

A general history of medieval ports along the North Sea and the Baltic has not yet been written. Research in the development of these harbours started in early 20th century with the study of late medieval written sources,[1] from which we learn that nearly all ports had been founded at the wrong places. Their problems arose from the insufficient depth of the rivers by which the seagoing ships had to get to them. As for the harbour installations such as jetties, quays, cranes or warehouses, the evidence from the port prospects of the 16th century throw a good deal of light on the subject. The loading and unloading of medieval ships seems to have been not unlike that of about 1900, but less effective.

In the 1950s Paul Johannsen at Hamburg was one of the first historians who, by studying the merchants' churches in the harbour areas, confronted his readers with quite another system of cargo handling.[2] At the same time German and Polish archaeologists published the first harbour excavations, which had been undertaken in the destroyed seaports after World War II.[3] About two decades later urban archaeology was got under way in the other countries around the North Sea and the Baltic. Here archaeologists excavated constructional details of harbour installations. In 1979 Brian Hobly and Gustav Milne invited specialists of these countries to discuss their results during the first international conference on 'waterfront archaeology' in London, which sparked a series of further international conferences in this field of research,[4] the last of them three weeks ago at Copenhagen. The proceedings of the conferences set international standards for dealing with the rather complicated archaeological sources.

As a result of all these efforts the historian who wants to study the development of medieval harbours finds himself in something like a jungle of fragmentary and disparate information from written, pictorial, archaeological and topographical sources. Above all, each port had its own individual ways of working which differ more or less from those of other ports, not only in the construction of jetties and quays, but even more in the organisation of cargo-handling and trade. To find a practicable way out of this confusing situation, a guideline is needed. I propose to take the organisation of trade as that guideline. The reason for this proposal is very simple: the harbour did not generate its trade, but the trade dictated the conditions under which harbours flourished or declined.

In the early Middle Ages seafaring merchants from different regions met at trading harbours, exchanged some of their merchandise among themselves and sold other parts of the cargo to the inhabitants of the harbour and its area. First of all a harbour of this kind had to offer the foreign merchants a large public market close to the landing places of the ships. The specific term for this type of market in an English document of the 9th century is in Latin: *'ripa emtoralis'*.[5] The German translation is *'Ufermarkt'*, the English equivalent might be 'harbour-market'. Each merchant who arrived there by sea wanted to erect his tent on the dry land as near to his ship as possible, to display his merchandise there and to cook hot meals for his crew, as they could not cook on board in those days. They slept in their tents at night-time and waited for customers in daytime. They visited the tents of the other merchants to exchange their goods. They sought a new supply of fresh water and fresh food and bought good fish directly from the local fishermen. As far as necessary they repaired their ships using the tools they had on board for this purpose. In their spare time they played at dice, nine men's morris and other board games, sang songs accompanied by harps and played the flute and, for sure, drank not only water. Traces of all these activities have been excavated from different harbour-markets.[6]

In Europe north of the Alps harbour-markets are much older than urban civilisation. Even in the Middle Ages harbour-markets could flourish far away from any town. It was often the other way round: many harbour-markets developed into medieval towns. Therefore archaeologists can only find undisturbed harbour-markets where these did not grow into towns. The most important excavation is still that of the Icelandic harbour-market of Gasar (Fig. 1), investigated at the beginning of this century.[7] Due to the hostile climate of that island, the merchants dug their tents deeply into the soil; thus the traces of these tents are to be seen all over the area. The ships landed by beaching and the merchants erected their tents in a long row parallel to the row of their beached ships. Further inland is another row of tents, namely those of the Icelanders, who came here from their farms for a couple of days to get continental goods in exchange for their own products.

In the background we see the foundations of the only stone building, a church fortified by a rampart. This rampart fulfilled the second demand which merchants made on harbour-markets: they needed security against any kind of threat. In case of danger, they took their precious goods and withdrew behind the rampart to defend themselves. In the context of security the church had at least three different functions. Continental merchants who visited Iceland in the Middle Ages normally had a priest with them who not only did their accounts, but said the mass for them in thanks

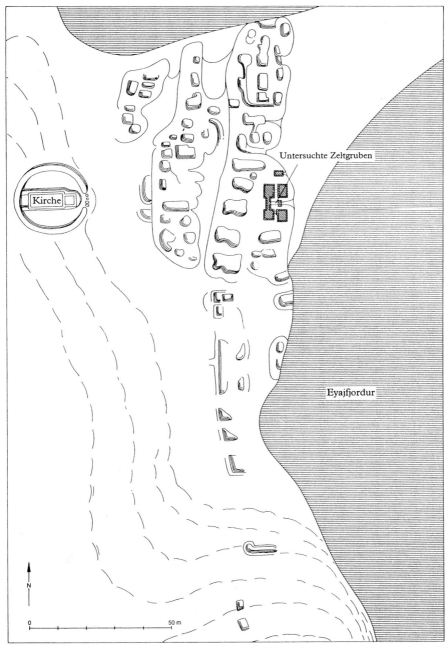

Fig. 1 Gasar, Iceland. Plan of the medieval harbour-market with the traces
of tents and a church surrounded by a rampart. *After D. Bruun.*

39

for a safe arrival and to pray for a safe return. Secondly, the strong and lockable stone building was used as a warehouse, which was additionally protected bypopular belief in the sin of sacrilege. Thirdly, the foreign merchants could be sure of a burial in consecrated earth if they died of illness or in hostile action.

Fig. 2 Harbour-market near the village of Lehe, now part of Bremerhaven.

f = Copper of W. Dilich 1603;
g = Chapel of the Holy Cross with cemetery for foreigners, both in a rampart;
h = ferry-house;
k = market place along the riverbank with market cross.

Except for the pits of the tents, the topography of the harbour-market at Gasar was not peculiar to Iceland but very common along the North Sea and the Baltic, as is seen in an engraving of 1603 which shows the harbour-market near the village of Lehe,[8] which is now a suburb of Bremerhaven (Fig.2). The church is surrounded by a rampart and up to the 19th century foreigners were buried in the churchyard. The market area stretched down to the bank of a small tidal river which, after some kilometres through many loops, flowed into the mouth of the river Weser. Seagoing vessels could reach the market on the rising tide and could similarly get out again. Their berths behind the loops of the river were protected against waves and storms. The ferry-house tells us that the market was also visited by people from the other side of the river.

40

The most interesting harbour installation is the market-cross, telling every foreign merchant that he could find there a market-judge who was able to rule on any case in commercial dispute, on the spot and finally. The merchant had to pay for the judgement, but could be sure that he would get it without delay and that it was executed forcibly if necessary. This was another element of security for the foreign merchant. Another cross, on top of his mast, was the widely visible declaration of the merchant that his ship came as a peaceful trading vessel. Important harbour towns, such as Antwerp, Bremen or Hamburg, throughout the Middle Ages erected a secondary cross on the riverbank several kilometres downstream of their town centre to tell incoming skippers that their trading vessels had reached the zone in which the town gave special protection for visitors to its market. A well organized harbour had to offer to seafaring merchants a market place frequented by many traders and a series of different facilities for security. Loading and unloading the ship remained more or less the problem of the merchant and his crew.

At Novgorod, the most important trading centre of medieval Russia, the large harbour-market is still to be seen along the right bank of the river Wolchow.[9] From there it extends to the top of a low hill, where the wide market-place is crowned by a series of merchants' churches.

And here in King's Lynn there were two different harbour-markets which remain busy commercial centres today (Fig. 3). As Helen Clarke stated twenty years ago,[10] Bishop Herbert of Norwich had founded the first harbour-market along the bank of the river in the late 11th century, together with the church of St Margaret. The market-place is the Saturday Market and the church is the parish and priory church of the town, which started to develop around the

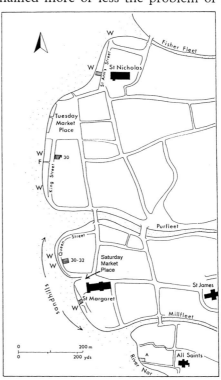

Fig. 3 Early King's Lynn (c.1050 c.1250) with two harbour-markets, one in front of St Margaret (Saturday Market), the other near St Nicholas (Tuesday Market). *After H. Clarke.*

41

market after its foundation. Inside this church two monumental brasses cover the tombs of two rich merchants who died in 1349 and in 1364. And inside the central lantern (destroyed in 1741) had been the coats of arms of many merchants. There is no doubt at all, that this church had been closely related to trade and merchants.

The second harbour-market had been founded further north on the riverbank by Bishop William of Norwich in the middle of the 12th century and is the Tuesday Market today which, down to the 19th century, had a market cross. Just to the north-east of the market, the chapel of St Nicholas had close links to merchants and seafarers, as is shown by bench ends with carved ships of the 15th century, by memorials of merchants and seafarers and by two brass fishes, the emblem of fishermen, at the south porch. The fishermen's quarter extended from St Nicholas to the Fisher Fleet. True's Yard Museum shows how fishermen worked and lived in the 19th and early 20th centuries.

Today both market places are cut off by houses from the riverbank, which originally served the markets with a series of staithes (Fig. 4). These houses were erected on reclaimed land from the silted riverbank. Many of the houses erected here fulfilled important functions in the commercial world of the late Middle Ages and the following centuries. For example, both the Hanseatic Steelyard and the neighbouring Hampton Court, with its arcades on the private quay at the former riverside, are close to St Margaret's and the Saturday Market, where the medieval Trinity Guildhall today serves as part of the Town Hall. Close to the Tuesday Market there is the late medieval St George's Guildhall, which originally had its own quay. The later Corn Exchange is in a similar position with one face to the river and the other to the same market, which is now surrounded by a remarkable assemblage of buildings, and is linked by a short street to the Common Staith where there was a big crane. There was also a ferry here, which took the inhabitants from the other side of the river to the market.

To sum up, both harbour markets of King's Lynn served as a focus of trade and other sea-based activities and, though they were cut off from the riverbank by rows of houses, which were erected on reclaimed land, in late medieval times, both markets continued under ever-changing conditions.

This development is in general very much in line with that of many other harbour-markets which grew to become trading towns. I give the example of Otterndorf,[11] a small town along the river Medem (Fig. 5), a small tributary of the lower Elbe, far enough from the main stream to be sheltered from waves and storms. Ships coming upstream first met the castle, which ensured the security and the summary justice of the harbour-market. Further south there is the church in the middle of the market place. And between church and river there is now one row of 17 houses, with their main

42

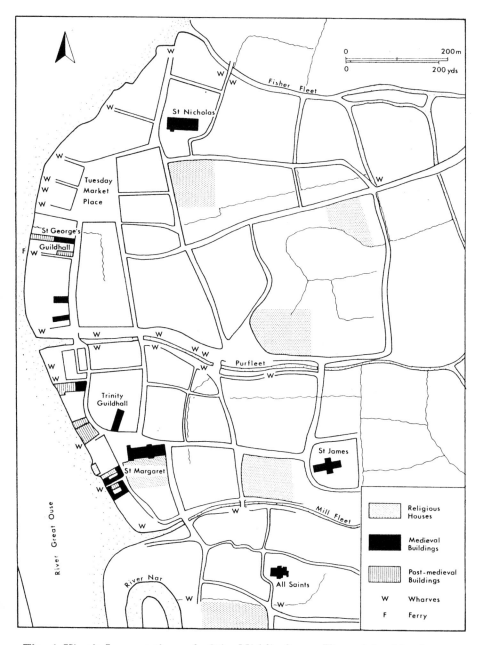

Fig. 4 King's Lynn at the end of the Middle Ages. The original harbour-markets are separated from the river by a row of private plots.

After H. Clarke.

43

fronts facing the market on a street running parallel to the river, and with their back doors facing the river. In these houses there lived 17 shippers and their families. On their small ships they landed directly at their own back doors or started from there with every kind of cargo. We have excavated in the small area between one house and the river and found some stairs leading down from the house to the river just like a corresponding scene in the tapestry of Bayeux. The foundation of the stairs was made from parts of the planking of a boat.

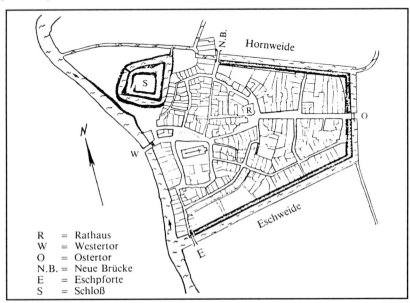

Fig. 5 Otterndorf, Kreis Cuxhaven. The original harbour-market with the church of St Severin separated from the river by a row of private plots.
After D. Ellmers 1986.

This situation is very typical in harbour towns that developed from harbour-markets. Like foreign merchants, who erected their tents along the riverbank of public harbour-markets, other merchants settled on private plots along the same riverbank downstream or upstream of the public market and, in the course of time, cut off the river from the public market. Seafaring merchants in these houses could collect the products of the town and of the surrounding country through the year and tranship them in their own vessels wherever they wanted. Their ships could moor at the back of their properties. That is the way in which the Hanseatic steelyards carried out their work in London as well as at King's Lynn with one face to the river and the other to a street running parallel to the river.

When in 1159 the harbour town of Lübeck in the southwest corner of the Baltic was founded (for the second time), its harbour was organized after the traditional pattern as a harbour market along the river,[12] after which the guild of the seafaring merchants named itself *'de mene kopman by de Travene'*, or the common merchants at the Trave. But, in spite of this traditional layout of the harbour, these merchants organized their trade in a new, forward-looking way.[13] Previously, merchants with carts travelling along the roads could not go to sea, and seafaring merchants who sailed their own ships could not travel along the roads. They had to meet at the harbour-markets to exchange their goods. Both groups, the land-travelling merchants from Westphalia and the seafarers in the tradition of the Frisians, had a better idea when Lübeck was founded. The seafarers became the companions of the land travellers and took them in their cogs from Lübeck to the other shores of the Baltic. The town seal of Lübeck[14] shows how the seafarer (with hooded coat) took the land-travelling merchant with him in his ship (fig. 6). Under the leadership of the Westphalians they bought exactly those

Fig. 6 The town seal of Lübeck (c.1250) shows a seafaring merchant and an overland merchant on board a cog. *After H. Ewe.*

goods which they could easily sell in Westphalia and at the end shared the profit. Both were the winners in this new type of collaboration: the Westphalians got to the sources of raw materials on the other shores of the Baltic and, when the seafarers arrived at Lübeck, they no longer had to wait for people to whom they could sell their merchandise. The Westphalians loaded the cargo onto their carts and travelled to the towns in their former homeland and sold the goods there. There was no need to exchange the merchandise at Lübeck, it just remained in the hands of the partnership which, in time, was named *'hanse'*.

For this new way of Hanseatic trade they soon found a useful wording: the Hanseatic merchant transported his goods over land and sea. Nearly the same wording is used in the name of a modern shipping company of a container-line, which reads as 'sea-land'. That is the same phenomenon: the container, too, is transported by ship across the sea and by lorry along the road or by railway, deep into the hinterland of a seaport. We all know how much the container changed the handling of cargo in the harbours of our times. The new way of Hanseatic trading, too, changed the handling of cargo in the late 12th and early 13th centuries. After a period of two generations the merchants of Lübeck found that they no longer needed a harbour-market and made better use of its area. They used it for merchants' houses, leaving just a narrow quay for loading and unloading of the ships, and built their city wall in between their houses and the quay.[15]

These changes in commercial practice had many different results:

1. First of all, in the harbour cities it was no longer the harbour-market but the individual houses of each merchant that became the centre of trade, where the merchandise was collected, stored and prepared for transhipment, where the trading partners met and planned new activities and from where the merchant himself, by ship or cart, carried his goods to distant ports or inland towns and returned home with foreign products. And when in the 14th century the merchant learned to read and write and direct the streams of goods by letters, he himself had no longer to travel but sat down every morning in his 'skrive kamere', his house more and more becoming the centre of expanding trade.[16]

2. These houses of the merchants were protected by a city wall not only from attacks along the land side but also along the waterside against enemies that might come in ships. The protection by ramparts or castles, into which the merchant could escape from enemies, was no longer available as it had been in the days of harbour-markets.

3. Consequently, all the cargo of a ship had to be carried through the harbour-gates or water-gates of the city wall (Fig. 7) to the houses of the merchants and, for this purpose, many new jobs were created:[17] different types of carriers, some for barrels with herring, others for sacks of grain, or for loading and unloading the ships. Then cart drivers had to take the goods from the quay to the houses of the merchants. Each harbour town, which adopted the new system, developed its own way of job-sharing. But the principle is clearly to be seen. The traditional harbour-market had been something like a self-service system, where the handling of the cargo was done by the crew of the seagoing merchant. The late medieval harbour lost

its market but became a service centre and for all the new services the merchant had to pay special taxes or other sums of money.

4. As the new system of trade caused a boom in the exchange and transhipment of goods, the merchants had no problems in paying for the new jobs. Thus many people could earn their living as harbour workers.

Fig. 7 Late medieval harbour town. There is no space for a harbour-market. The merchandise has to be carried from the ships through the gates in the city wall to the houses of the merchants and vice versa.
Woodcut of Schöffer 1523.

5. The merchants were interested in controlling the weight of special cargoes and installed large weighing machines at the quaysides and paid for them too.[18]

6. Another result of booming trade was the founding in the 13th century of new Hanseatic seaports especially along the southern coast of the Baltic. And all these new towns more or less copied the topography of Lübeck without any harbour-market. The market in the centre of the towns served just for what the citizens needed every day, not for long distance trade.

7. Old seaports with harbour-markets found individual methods of adopting the new system. Bremen, for example, converted its old harbour-market into a market for daily goods before the middle of the 13th century and constructed a new quay along the main stream of the river Weser without a market area.[19] Other harbour towns, especially those inland, instead of the open harbour-market, from *c.*1300 erected public warehouses at their waterfronts. Inside, merchandise could be stored, exchanged and prepared for transportation, all under the shelter of a roof and under the control of the city government.[20]

Another result of the booming trade from the 1180s was that most merchants ordered bigger ships from the shipyards and, of course, got them, but this created new problems which they had to solve:

1. First, shipbuilding became an urban profession with high standards, as ships in every harbour town were the main means of transport. Ships needed to be as large as required by the merchants and as secure and as cheap as possible. But space was needed for their production, and each harbour town had to decide where along the waterfront this important work should be undertaken, including the repair of vessels returning from long voyages.

2. The Middle Ages are often looked upon as backward, with little or no progress in technical developments, but shipwrights were so creative that towards the end of this period the European ship had developed considerably and made possible a network of worldwide trade.[21]

3. In the late Middle Ages ships became bigger, had deeper holds and deeper draught and needed quay-constructions with greater depth. In front of the old quay the craftsmen rammed poles into deeper water and, in the course of time, the quays step by step grew into the river. The construction of quays became a sophisticated profession.[22]

4. The deeper the hold of a ship the more difficult it was to take the goods out of the ship. In the middle of the 13th century harbour cranes for the first time became a permanent installation at the ports. In the Ancient Mediterranean, moveable cranes were used in harbours for very heavy items of cargo and taken away when the ship was unloaded. Since the late Middle Ages cranes have been a typical and permanent feature of any harbour. As for the different types of cranes, I will not go into details here.[23]

5. Seaports were founded in the 12th or 13th centuries at places easily reached by ships of that time, but were later confronted with problems caused by the growth in the size of ships. Bruges faced such problems, for example. Such seaports built harbours further downstream or tried to deepen the rivers by narrowing their beds with special dams and wooden constructions.[24]

In the second quarter of the 13th century seaports started to erect seamarks to guide ships to the harbour entrances, especially at the mouths of rivers.[25]

In the early 14th century these seamarks acquired lanterns and in the early 15th century the first buoys were laid out. Money was collected from ships' captains for all these services that the seaports arranged for them.[26]

To sum up, we clearly see the results of concentrating the organization of long-distance trade in the houses of the merchants. Trade grew and many

48

technical problems had to be solved. This was much more than any single merchant could do. Each harbour town needed to set up a municipal body able to undertake commercial operations on behalf of the whole community.

Notes

[1] Walther Vogel, Geschichte der deutschen Seeschiffahrt Bd. 1, 1915, pp. 532-539.

[2] Paul Johannsen, chapter 'Die Kaufmannskirche' in his article 'Umrisse und Aufgaben der hansischen Siedlungsgeschichte und Kartographie', *Hansische Geschichtsblätter* 73, 1955, pp. 1-105, here pp. 37-40. - Ders, Die Kaufmannskirche im Ostseegebiet, in: *Vorträge und Forschungen IV, Studien zu den Anfängen des europäischen Städtewesens*, ed. by Th. Mayer, Lindau-Konstanz 1958, p. 499-525. - Ders, Die Kaufmannskirche, in: *Die Zeit der Stadtgründungen im Ostseeraum*. Acta Visbyensia I, Visby-symposiet för historisca vetenskaper 1963. Visby 1965, pp. 85-134.

[3] Summarized in: Detlev Ellmers, *Frühmittelalterliche Handelsschiffahrt in Mittel- und Nordeuropa*, Neumünster 1972, pp. 123-226.

[4] *Waterfront Archaeology in Britain and Northern Europe*, ed. by Gustav Milne and Brian Hobly. CBA Research Report No. 41 1981. - *Conference on Waterfront Archaeology in North European Towns* No. 2, Bergen 1983, ed. by Asbjørn E. Herteig, Bergen 1985. - *Waterfront Archaeology*. Proceedings of the Third International Conference, Bristol 1988, ed. by G.L. Good, R.H. Jones and M.W. Ponsford. CBA Research Report No. 74, London 1991.

[5] Detlev Ellmers (like note 3) p. 225. - W. Birch, *Cartularium Saxonicum*, 1897, no. 561, 577, 578.

[6] Detlev, Ellmers, 'Die Verlagerung des Fernhandels vom öffentlichen Ufermarkt in die privaten Häuser der Kaufleute', Lübecker Schriften zur Archäologie und Kulturgeschichte (LSAK) 20, 1990, pp. 101-108. - Manfred Gläser, 'Der Lübecker Ufermarkt und die angrenzende Bebauung'. Die Ausgrabungen auf den Grundstücken Alfstraße 36/38, LSAK 17, 1988, pp. 125-129. - Ingrid Schalies, 'Erkenntnisse der Archäologie zur Geschichte des Lübecker Hafens', LSAK 17, 1988, pp. 129-132.

[7] Finnur Jónsson og Daniel Bruun, Det gamle handelssted Gásar (ad Gásum), yngre Gaesir, ved Øfjord. Undersøgelser foretagne i sommeren 1907. Oversigt over det Kgl. Danske Videnskabernes selskabs forhandlinger 1908 No. 3, pp. 95-111, fig. I-VIII. - Reviewed by Edward Schröder, in: Hansische Geschichtsblätter 1908, pp. 473-475. - Detlev Ellmers (like note 3) p. 215f., fig. p. 222f.

[8] Detlev Ellmers, Der mittelalterliche Hafen von Lehe. Jahrbuch der Männer vom Morgenstern, Bremerhaven, 62, 1983, pp. 45-72. - Detlev Ellmers, Der Leher Hafen im Mittelalter. In: Lina Delfs, Schiffahrt auf der Geeste (= Schriften des Deutschen Schiffahrtsmuseums vol. 17) 1986, pp. 172-185.

[9] Konrad Onasch, *Großnowgorod und das Reich der heiligen Sophia*, Leipzig 1969, pp. 69-75.

[10] Helen Clarke, 'The medieval waterfront of King's Lynn'. In: *Waterfront Archaeology in Britain and Northern Europe*, ed. by Gustav Milne and Brian Hobly. CBA Research Report No. 41, 1981, pp. 132-135.

[11] Detlev, Ellmers, 'Hafenanlagen in Stade. Fragen und Probleme'. In: *Auf den Spuren des alten Stade*. Stade 1986, pp. 47-58, here p. 51f.

[12] See note 6.

[13] Detlev Ellmers, *Die Entstehung der Hanse*, Hansische Geschichtsblätter 103, 1985, pp. 3-40.

[14] Herbert Ewe, Schiffe auf Siegeln, Bielefeld 1972, p. 147.

[15] See note 6.

[16] Fritz Rörig, *Die europäische Stadt im Mittelalter*, Göttingen 1955, p. 25.

[17] Matthijs van der Velden, *Hafenarbeit und Trägergilden. Ein Beitrag zur Arbeits-organisation in See- und Flußhäfen vor 1850.* Rotterdam 1998.

[18] Detlev Ellmers, 'Kran und Waage im Hafen'. In: *Vom rechten Maß der Dinge. Beiträge zur Wirtschafts- und Sozialgeschichte. Festschrift für Harald Witthöft* zum 65. Geburtstag, St. Katharinen 1996, pp. 145-165.

[19] Ulrich Weidinger, *Mit Koggen zum Markplatz. Bremens Hafenstrukturen vom frühen Mittelalter bis zum Beginn der Industrialisierung,* Bremen 1997.

[20] Harald Witthöft, *Das Kaufhaus in Lüneburg,* Lüneburg 1962.

[21] Detlev Ellmers and Uwe Schnall, 'Schiffbau und Schiffstypen im mittelalterlichen Europa, in: Europäische Technik im Mittelalter 800 bis 1400', *Tradition und Innovation. Ein Handbuch,* ed. by Uta Lindgren, Berlin 1996, pp. 350-370. - Detlev Ellmers, 'Wikingerschiffe, Koggen, Holken und Dreimaster. Menschen auf See im Mittelalter', in: *Mensch und Natur im mittelalterlichen Europa.* Akten der Akademie Friesach 'Stadt und Kultur im Mittelalter', Friesach (Kärnten), 1.-5. September 1997, ed. by Konrad Spindler, Klagenfurt 1998, pp. 101-128.

[22] Detlev Ellmers, *Von der Schiffslände zum Hafenbecken.* Hafenbautechnik an der Nord- und Ostsee von den Anfängen bis sum ausgehenden Mittelalter, Jahrbuch der Hafen-bautechnischen Gesellschaft 40, 1983/84, pp. 5-19. -Detlev Ellmers, 'Hafenbau, in: Europäische Technik im Mittelalter 800 bis 1400', *Tradition und Innovation. Ein Handbuch,* ed. by Uta Lindgren, Berlin 1996, pp. 105-110.

[23] Detlev Ellmers, 'Development and Usage of Harbour Cranes', in: *Medieval ships and the birth of technological societies, vol. 1, Northern Europe,* Malta 1989, pp. 43-69. - Michael Matheus, *Hafenkrane. Zur Geschichte einer Maschine am Rhein und seinen Nebenflüssen von Straßburg bis Düsseldorf,* Trier 1985.

[24] See note 1.

[25] Detlev Ellmers, 'Das Hafenzeichen von Travemünde', in: *Lübeck 1226. Reichsfreiheit und frühe Stadt.* Lübeck 1976, pp. 57-61. - John Naish, *Seamarks. Their History and Development.* London 1985.

[26] Uwe Schnall, 'Navigationstechniken', in: *Europäische Technik im Mittelalter 800 bis 1400, Tradition und Innovation. Ein Handbuch,* ed. by Uta Lindgren, Berlin 1996, pp. 373-380. - Arend W. Lang, *Entwicklung, Aufbau und Verwaltung des Seezeichenwesens an der deutschen Nordseeküste bis zur Mitte des 19. Jahrhunderts,* Bonn 1965. - Kurt Ferber, *Die Entwicklung des Hamburger Tonnen-, Baken -und Leuchtfeuerwesens, Zeitschrift des Vereins für hamburgische Geschichte* 18, 1913, 1-102.

MERCHANTS AND TRADE

Trade and Merchants from Lynn in the Baltic Ports at the End of the 16th Century and in the First Half of the 17th Century

by

Andrzej Groth

Towns (and other geographical) names particularly of the east Baltic region are in the spelling of the 16th century as found in the sources, e.g. Danzig, Elbing, Königsberg, Pillau. Towns (and other) names in connection with modern authorities or institutions are in modern spelling (Polish, Lithuanian) e.g. Archiwum, Panstwowe, Gdansk, port authorities Elblag, Kaliningrad.

The question of trade between the English port of Lynn and the ports of the southern Baltic, because of a lack of relevant sources, will have to be confined to contacts between Lynn and Elbing.[1] The surviving customs records from Königsberg between 1549 and 1645 (Geheimes Staatsarchiv Preußischer Kulturbesitz, Berlin) record neither the loading port of the ships nor their destination. It is, therefore, impossible to get information on the geographic direction of Königsberg's foreign trade. A similar situation exists in the case of the Danzig customs records. The Pfahlzollregister as preserved in Archiwum Panstwowe from 1634, 1640 and 1641, as well as those from the second half of the 18th century, give no information concerning the loading port of the ships nor their destination.[2] Both sets of records, the Königsberg as well as those from Gdansk, merely tell us the place of residence of the shipper, which is not the same as the loading port of the ship or the destination of its cargo.

The main source used in this paper is the collection of thirty-five customs record books from Elbing covering 1585-1587, 1594, 1596-1597, 1599-1607, 1612, 1615-1616, 1618-1620, 1623, 1625, 1653-1655, 1666, 1685, 1687, 1690-1691, 1695-1700.[3] They contain the first name and surname of the shipper, his place of residence, the date of entry into and departure from the port, the name and amount of cargo carried, the port of destination (in the case of exports from Elbing) or the loading port (in the case of imports). This enables research to be conducted into the geographical directions of the maritime trade of Elbing.

51

In Elbing, ships as well as goods imported and exported by sea were twice registered. The Geheime Staatsarchiv Preußischer Kulturbesitz also preserves the customs accounts of Pillau (Pilawa). They are compiled in 69 archive units for 1638 to 1712.[4]

A shipper calling at any port of the Frisches Haff [the large lagoon giving access to these harbours] - Elbing (Elblag), Braunsberg (Braniewo), Frauenburg (Frombork), only Königsberg (Kaliningrad) was excepted - was obliged to stop his ship when entering the Haff at Pillau and to report his arrival to the clerk of the customs chamber. The cargo was then examined and the shipper had to declare the nature of his cargo before the ship could continue on her way to the destination port. On his way back the shipper had to deliver a certificate with information about the kind and quantity of the goods discharged as well as any cargo loaded in the harbours mentioned above. This certificate had to be stamped with the seal of the town concerned and was the necessary evidence for the customs receipt and the entrance into the customs account book for the harbours. The information the Pillau customs collectors were interested in went much further than that found in the Danzig or Königsberg customs books. In the Pillau Chamber of Customs, not only entries such as name and surname, residence, dates of arrival and departure, kind and amount of the goods were usually registered, but additional information, most importantly, about the port of departure and of destination.

I think the Elbing and Pillau customs accounts are the most appropriate sources to investigate Elbing's sea trade and its connections with other ports. This seems confirmed if seen in comparison with the Sound Toll Registers. In 1616, for instance, the Sound Chamber of Customs registered the arrival of 12 ships from Elbing whose home harbour was Hull; on the other hand, 17 sail ships from Hull were entered in the Elbing customs books, three of which completed their cargo in Königsberg, one in Braunsberg and one in Danzig. In the same year, four ships were registered in the Sound whose home port was Newcastle, but the Elbing register noted 12 such ships, all of which took additional cargo in other harbours of the Frisches Haff. Ships with the home port of London, too, happened to be registered differently in the Sound and in Elbing. Again, in 1616, six ships coming from Elbing were registered in the Sound. But according to the Elbing customs accounts 21 ships left Elbing, 16 of which completed their cargo in Königsberg or in the Pillau 'Seetief'. These differences result from the fact that the goods from Elbing were brought in 'Schmacken' and 'Bordingen' (smaller ships for short distance transport) to the sail ships waiting in the Pillau Tief or in Königsberg. In these cases, the Sound register did not declare Elbing as the departure port, but that port from which the bulk of the cargo came. Statements based on the Sound Chamber Register may, in connection with

Elbing or Königsberg maritime trade, be totally misleading. These are some of the reasons why I did not include them in this paper.

Until 1580, English Baltic trade was largely confined to contacts with Danzig. For instance, between 1562 and 1579, 75% of English ships heading west out of the Baltic sailed out of the port of Danzig. Within the period mentioned, only 5 ships in 1577 left Elbing when Danzig harbour was blockaded by the Polish King Stefan Batory who, at the same time, ordered the transfer of raft timber transportation on the Weichsel from Danzig to Elbing. This situation changed radically with the formation of the English Eastland Company, the granting to this company by Queen Elizabeth I of monopoly rights to Baltic trade, and the decree issued in January 1580 by the English Privy Council that ships leaving London, Hull, Ipswich and Lynn for the Baltic should be unloaded exclusively in Elbing. Now Elbing became the sole storage place of English goods on the Baltic, although in fact the total removal of English merchants from Danzig to Elbing only took place in 1583 as the result of the signing of an appropriate agreement between the Eastland Company and Elbing municipal authorities. The port of Danzig's share in the shipping trade with England fell in the years 1580-1600 to 15.5% according to the Sound register. The role of Elbing, however, increased; 70.2% of English ships leaving the Baltic in this period departed from its harbour. The Elbinger Pfahlbücher 1585 to 1625 records an average of 70 sail ships a year bound from Elbing for Scottish and English harbours, or more than 50% of the ships leaving Elbing. The years 1585-1587 probably saw the most frequent contacts between Elbing and English and Scottish harbours. In these years, an annual average of 101 ships called from England and Scotland, or 68% of all ships leaving Elbing.

The Polish-Swedish War (1626-1629) drastically affected shipping and trade between England and Elbing. From the time when the Swedes occupied Elbing in 1626, the Eastland Company was deprived of the possibility of trade with the Republic of Poland. The Constitution of the Polish Parliament of 1628 deprived the Eastland Company of its earlier privileges in consequence of the company's co-operation with the Swedes in Elbing. The same order restored the monopoly on the trade in English cloth to Danzig.

The English tried to compensate for these losses by increasing their trade with Sweden, but this proved rather unprofitable, as Sweden was not able to absorb English goods in sufficient quantity.[5] Furthermore, Danzig opposed English and Scottish trade with Sweden. The heads of the Eastland Company estimated their losses during the Polish-Swedish War at more than £100,000.

The closure of the English commercial headquarters in Elbing impacted adversely on English-Elbingian trade connections. In 1638, the Elbing turnover in trade with English harbours fell back to one third of the mercantile value of the Eastland Company activities in Elbing. In the 1640s, the turnover of trade with England decreased to 4-6% of its value in 1594; the average number of ships leaving Elbing bound for English harbours was 5-7 a year, and this remained the case until the late seventies of the 17th century. Within the next decade the turnover value went down to a fraction of that in the years of the Eastland Company in Elbing. In the 1690s, shipping as well as trade connections between the two partners more or less came to an end.[6]

With the English residence in Elbing abandoned, the English/Baltic trade was transferred to Danzig, Königsberg and partly to Livonic harbours. From the seventies of the 17th century the main part of the trade was directed to Sweden.[7]

Against this background, what was the character of shipping and trade contacts between Elbing and Lynn?

The greatest density of shipping on the Lynn-Elbing-Lynn route was noted in the years 1586-1587. At this time 31 ships came to Elbing and left with cargoes destined for Lynn (12.9% of all ships leaving Elbing for English ports: 1586 - 13 ships, 1587 - 18 ships), and 52.5% of the total shipping between Elbing and Lynn. Lynn's activities (and partly those of other English harbours) should be seen in connection with the desperate situation of England in 1586-87 caused by bad harvests. Numerous sailing ships were sent to the Baltic to be loaded with grain which was so much in demand in England. In 1587, English grain import was at its highest level for the second half of the 16th century, that is 6,383 lasts of rye and 509 lasts of wheat, nearly all of it imported from Danzig, Elbing and Königsberg.[8] In 1586-87, the freight of the ships from Elbing destined for Lynn, was mainly grain: in all, 431 lasts of rye and 24 lasts of wheat, nearly 85% of the rye and 100% of the wheat that was sent between 1585 and 1625 from Elbing to Lynn. Seventeen of the 31 ships from Lynn to Elbing sailed in ballast. These ships were freighted on their return journey with grain. Five captains did not find what they were looking for in Elbing and consequently called at Königsberg or Danzig. After 1587, the movement of ships between Lynn and Elbing fell away to 1-2 ships a year (except 1602-03); this was 1.2 - 4% of the English ships calling at Elbing before the trade ended altogether in 1625.

In the period 1594-1625, 25 ships sailed from Lynn to Elbing, 4 of them in ballast, and 25 from Elbing to Lynn, 2 of them partly freighted and 7 in ballast. The latter shippers declared in the Elbing Customs Chamber they were going to look for freight in Königsberg or Danzig.

The decline in shipping and trade between Elbing and Lynn after 1587 was partly caused by problems at the port of Elbing: the less effective communication system with the hinterland compared with Danzig, and the double duty payable on goods coming into and leaving Elbing, in Pillau and

54

Elbing itself. Another contributing factor affecting trade between the two towns was that merchants from Lynn could not compete in terms of capital with the wholesalers from London and Hull.

Trade on the Lynn-Elbing route was mostly served by ships whose home port was Lynn. The Elbing market could not meet the English demand so the turnover between English harbours and Elbing decreased.

Only two ships (1596 and 1600) were registered with Dutch home ports (Enkhuizen and Rijp), four ships (1599, 1601, 1602, 1605) with Yarmouth and five from Scottish harbours (Kirkalde 4, St Andrea 1).

The ships on the Lynn-Elbing route called at Elbing once a year. Only in the particularly busy years on this route (1586-1587) did some ships come twice (1586 ship *Gersabe*, shipper Edward Brian; ship *Mai Flor*, shipper Benjamin Korck; ship *Maria Rose*, shipper William Buttlade; 1587 ship *Der Adler*, shipper Brian Lubkins; ship *Der Hirsch*, shipper Ritker Obermann).

The trade turnover between Elbing and Lynn (apart from the period 1586-1587) was also insignificant. Between 1594 and 1620 (these years are documented by customs taxes which allow estimates) Lynn's share in the total turnover of English and Scottish trade was between 0.4% and 1.3%. London, Hull and Newcastle had the greatest shares in this commerce.

In the cargoes coming from Lynn to Elbing, leather and skins, particularly sheep and rabbit skins, made up the greatest percentage. From 1585 to 1625, 981,500 grey and 22,925 black rabbit furs, 115,850 sheep skins and a small number of fox skins (91) and calf skins (80), were brought to Elbing. Apart from these items, merchants from Lynn sent great amounts (151,150 pieces) of tanned white leather to Elbing.

In spite of the considerable quantities of skins sent from Lynn to Elbing, their value was not very impressive because these were mostly raw skins, the price of which was not very high.

Among other goods carried from Lynn were textiles, which were a key commodity in the trade with Baltic cities. In the period 1585-1625, cloth constituted 90% of English imports to Elbing. In these years, 397 broad cloths *(gemeine Lundisch)*, preferred by Polish noblemen and the well-to-do, 1,565 pieces of the cheaper kerseys and 12 of the cheapest species ('dozens') came from Lynn to Elbing along with some black cloth *('laken')*, English Bays, and the so-called 'Rolltuch' and some lace and hose. In later periods the amount of cloth sent from Lynn to Elbing was very small indeed and the trade was of an occasional character. Eighteen barrels of train or fish oil and some wine complete this list of goods brought to Elbing in these years.

Exports from Elbing to Lynn were mainly raw materials and covered a group of approximately 22 articles. The dominant position, similar to that of the exports to England generally, was occupied by materials essential in the shipbuilding industry: pitch (6,452 lasts), tar (219 lasts), flax (176 lasts), hemp (15½ lasts), wood *('klapholt'* and prefabricated goods). Before the Polish-Swedish War (1626-1629), the English imported their wood chiefly from Danzig, later from Königsberg and Riga. Another important export to Lynn was iron (163 shippound) and ashes which were used at that time for dyeing and in the production of glass and soap.

Some manufactured commodities, too, were sent from Elbing to Lynn such as blankets, *'Kabelgarn'*, wooden dishes and linen. But these were in small quantities and only occasional exports, as was fish (eel, sturgeon).

The export of grain from Elbing to Lynn, like that to the other English harbours, was unusual. England was essentially self-sufficient in grain; so larger amounts were only imported when home production fell. In 1586-1587 there was a crop failure, so over 85% of all the rye and 100% of the wheat exported from Elbing to Lynn in the years 1585-1625 was sent in this short period. In the remaining years the export of grain from Elbing to Lynn was insignificant and occasional (total 77 lasts).

The Elbing customs books do not give too much information on Lynn merchants trading with Elbing. From 1587 to 1602, the name of John Wollmann is mentioned, a Lynn merchant who, in 1587, sent 41 pieces of broadcloth and, in 1602, 12,000 rabbit skins to Elbing. In 1587 he exported from Elbing 21 lasts of flax, 38 shippound of iron and 9 barrels of ashes. He kept trade contacts with Königsberg too. The Lynn merchant, Peter Plan, sent 166 pieces of norderkersey, 21,000 rabbit skins and 4,000 pieces of tanned white leather to Elbing; Stefan Lacktoh, in 1587, exported 18 lasts of pitch, 8 lasts of tar and 3 lasts of flax from Elbing to Lynn; William Marshal, in 1587, exported 12 shippound of iron, 40 stones of feathers, 29 lasts of ashes, 5 lasts of flax, 60 quarters of sturgeon; Thomas Densen imported 216 pieces of norderkersey to Elbing and exported 13½ lasts of rye from this harbour; Robert Kelle, in 1587, brought 18 lasts of pitch and 20 lasts of tar from Elbing to Lynn. In 1596, one of the participants in Lynn/Elbing trade was the London merchant John Philips who exported 18 lasts of tar, 18 lasts of pitch, 5 lasts of flax and 20 shock (shock = three score) of wooden dishes or plates to Lynn. In 1598 three Lynn merchants - we do not know their names - were busy in Baltic trade: they despatched eastward 9 pieces of broadcloth and 72,000 rabbit skins and, from Elbing westward, 40 great-hundreds of wood or *klapholt* and 1½ greathundred *wagenschoß* (half-finished wooden boards and planks cut ready for use).[9]

The crew members aboard the ships on the Lynn/Elbing route had business with Elbing on their own account. The total of their goods exported from Lynn to Elbing was 1.6% of the white leather, 0.4% of the sheep skins, 0.1% of the rabbit skins and, from Elbing to Lynn, 5.2% of the rye, 4.7% of the flax, 4.5% of the ashes, 4.7% of the pitch and 0.9% of the tar.

Table 1. Ships' traffic on a route from Elblag to Lynn 1585-1625

National Record Office in Gdansk (AP Gd), Record Office of Elblag 369, 1 no 2828-2850

SHIPS SAILED OUT OF ELBLAG FOR ENGLISH & SCOTTISH PORTS	---------------SHIPS SAILED FOR LYNN----------------				
YEAR	Number	Number fully-loaded	Number partly-loaded	Number with ballast	Total	%
1585	60	3	-	-	3	5.0
1586	131	11	1	1	13	9.9
1587	113	12	2	4	18	15.9
1594	76	1	-	-	1	1.3
1596	69	1	-	-	1	1.4
1597	81	1	-	-	1	1.2
1599	69	1	-	-	1	1.4
1600	65	2	-	-	2	3.1
1601	67	2	-	-	2	3.0
1602	42	2	-	1	3	7.1
1603	48	1	-	-	1	2.1
1605	55	2	-	-	2	3.6
1607	75	1	-	-	1	1.3
1612	67	-	-	1	1	1.5
1615	83	-	-	1	1	1.2
1616	72	-	-	1	1	1.4
1618	71	-	-	1	1	1.4
1619	73	1	-	-	1	1.4
1620	54	1	1	-	2	3.7
1623	53	-	-	1	1	1.9
1625	49	-	1	1	2	4.1

Table 2. Participation of English and Scottish ports in trade turnover of Elblag (%)

National Record Office in Gdansk (AP Gd), Record Office of Elblag 369, 1 no 2830, 2832, 2834-2836, 2844-2848, 2857, 2861-2866, 2870, 2881-2891; Record Office in Gdansk (AP Gd), 300,19 no 45[1-2], 45[5-7], 45[13], 45[18a], 45[19-20], 45[20a], 45[22-23]; Geheimes Staatsarchiv Preussischer Kulturbesitz Berlin, Ostpreussische Foliaten, no 12909-12974.

PORT	1594	1597	1599	1600	1615	1616	1618	1619	1620
London	66.0	64.4	68.9	49.2	47.8	40.2	54.1	37.5	32.8
Hull	18.8	20.0	15.8	30.8	25.4	25.5	34.5	39.6	40.5
Newcastle	3.4	8.6	2.3	3.4	15.9	10.2	9.9	14.0	18.8
Ipswich	6.5	4.9	6.6	11.8	9.7	13.7	0.5	8.6	7.0
Lynn	0.7	-	0.4	1.3	0.4	0.5	1.0	0.5	0.9
Harwich	4.6	0.5	0.6	-	0.8	9.9	-	-	-
Jersey	-	0.1	-	-	-	-	-	-	-
Abroch	-	1.5	2.5	-	-	-	-	-	-
Yarmouth	-	-	0.9	0.3	-	-	-	-	-
Kirkalde	-	-	0.1	-	-	-	-	-	-
York	-	-	1.9	3.2	-	-	-	-	-
Leith	-	-	-	-	-	-	-	-	-

PORT	1638	1647	1648	1664	1668	1673	1674	1675	1676
London	56.6	26.3	46.9	30.5	43.7	100.0	13.7	21.2	45.2
Hull	39.2	70.3	40.8	55.9	55.4	-	37.8	58.2	28.9
Newcastle	4.1	0.5	-	13.6	0.9	-	48.5	20.6	25.9
Ipswich	0.1	0.4	5.7	-	-	-	-	-	-
Lynn	-	-	-	-	-	-	-	-	-
Harwich	-	-	-	-	-	-	-	-	-
Jersey	-	-	-	-	-	-	-	-	-
Abroch	-	-	-	-	-	-	-	-	-
Yarmouth	-	-	-	-	-	-	-	-	-
Kirkalde	-	-	-	-	-	-	-	-	-
York	-	-	-	-	-	-	-	-	-
Leith	-	2.5	6.6	-	-	-	-	-	-

PORT	1677	1683	1686	1690	1694	1695	1696	1698	1700
London	23.0	-	20.4	100.0	-	-	-	-	100.0
Hull	46.4	100.0	22.0	-	-	-	-	-	-
Newcastle	30.6	-	57.6	-	-	-	-	-	-
Ipswich	-	-	-	-	-	-	-	-	-
Lynn	-	-	-	-	-	-	-	-	-
Harwich	-	-	-	-	-	-	-	-	-
Jersey	-	-	-	-	-	-	-	-	-
Abroch	-	-	-	-	-	-	-	-	-
Yarmouth	-	-	-	-	-	-	-	-	-
Kirkalde	-	-	-	-	-	-	-	-	-
York	-	-	-	-	-	-	-	-	-
Leith	-	-	-	-	-	-	-	-	-

Table 3. Ships and skippers taking part in the shipping trade on a route from Elbing to Lynn

YEAR	SKIPPER'S NAME	SHIP'S NAME	HOME PORT
1585	Thomas Mallebe	*David*	Lynn
	Brian Lubkins	*The Eagle (Der Adler)*	Lynn
1586	Edwert Brian	*Gersabe*	Lynn
	John Schwanson	*Anna Ballaendt*	Lynn
	William Kutson	*Mai Flor*	Lynn
	Benjamin Korck	*Maria Rose*	Lynn
	Corneli Moor	*The Pearl (Die Perle)*	Lynn
	Thomas Bertkorck	*The Black Lamb (Der Schwarze Lamm)*	Lynn
	John Duck	*David*	Lynn
	John Tomlyn	*The White Bear (Der weise Bär)*	Lynn
	Brian Lubkins	*The Eagle (Der Adler)*	Lynn
1587	Robert Waal	*William*	Lynn
	Thomas Palmars	*William*	Lynn
	William Blacket	*The Young Swan (Der Junge Schwan)*	Lynn
	William Buttlade	*Salamander*	Lynn
	Peter Mathen	*Berckschmiedt*	Lynn
	Brian Lubkins	*The Eagle (Der Adler)*	Lynn
	Thomas Atken	*William*	Lynn
	Thomas Bylbe	*Jesus*	Lynn
	Ritker Obermann	*The Stag (Der Hirsch)*	Lynn
	Ritker Grayss	*Maria Jarmann*	Lynn
	Ritker Hardeck	*Haumagt*	Lynn
	John Duck	*David*	Lynn
	John Tamlyn	*The White Bear (Der weise Bär)*	Lynn
	Thomas Foderston	*David*	Lynn
	George Altkirch	*George*	Lynn
	Thomas Bardinar	*Maria Rosa*	Lynn
1594	Rittger Bittings	*Der Christopherus*	Lynn
1596	Claus Janssen	*The Dragon (Der Drach)*	Enkhuizen
1598	Richard Hadock	*John Magdt*	Lynn
1599	Andreas Mastertos	*Maria Catherina*	Kirkcaldy
1600	John Turckell	*The Hopeful (Die Hoffewohl)*	Lynn
	Claus Janns	*?*	Rijp
1601	David Hay	*Timotheus*	Kirkcaldy
	George Hay	*The Nightingale (Der Nachtigall)*	Kirkcaldy
1602	Thomas Burfurtt	*George*	Lynn
	William Cuper	*The Benediction (Der Segen)*	Yarmouth
	John Wollman	*George*	Lynn
1603	John Breyde	*Antelope (Antilopa)*	Lynn
1605	Jacob Braun	*Gratia Dei*	Kirkcaldy
	Patrick Muffet	*Providentia*	S. Andrea
1607	Richard Bittings	*Nary (Der Mehriweib)*	Lynn

1612	Richard Bittings	*Margaret (Margareta)*	Lynn
1615	Robert Commistable	*Dolphin (Delphin)*	Lynn
1616	John Junge	*John Baptist (Johann Baptista)*	Lynn
1619	Wieledt Dreinford	*Anna*	Lynn
1620	John Junge	*Dolphin (Delphin)*	Lynn
	John Stanton	*The Globe (Globus)*	Lynn
1623	Wieledt Dreinford	*The Fiddler (Der Wioll)*	Lynn
1625	Robert Hawardt	*Anna*	Lynn
	Richard Lemon	*Lemon*	Lynn

Table 4. Imports from Lynn to Elbing during 1585-1625

National Record Office in Gdansk (AP Gd), Record Office of Elblag 369, 1 no 2828-2850

ARTICLE	UNIT OF MEASURE	NUMBER
Textiles		
North dozens	Piece	12
North kersey	Piece	1207
Common kersey	Piece	358
Common broadcloth	Piece	397
Black broadcloth	Piece	3
Narrow bay	Piece	15
Roltuch	Piece	8
Haberdashery		
Trimming	Ell	800 [a]
Woollen stockings	Dozen	376 [b]
Leathers & Pelts		
Grey cony skin	Piece	981,500
Black cony skin	Piece	22,925
White leather	Piece	151,150
Lamb-skin	Piece	115850
Fox-pelt	Piece	91
Calf-leather	Ten	8
Other Articles		
Wine	Bot	6
"	Oxhoft	1
Malaga wine	Pipen	8
Cod-liver oil	Tonne	18

[a] 25 florins value
[b] 1919 florins value

Table 5. Exports from Elbing to Lynn

National Record Office in Gdansk (AP Gd), Record Office of Elblag 369, 1 no 2828-2850,

ARTICLE	UNIT OF MEASURE	NUMBER
Corn		
Rye	Last	508¼
Wheat	Last	24
Flour	Last	7½
Other agricultural products		
Flax	Last	176
"	Stones	27
Hemp	Last	15½
Feathers	Stones	190
Forest products		
Stave	Rings	21½
Wagenshos	Piece	60
Pitch	Last	645½
Birch Tar	Last	219
Ash	Last	166½
"	Fass	11
Wax	Schippound (Schiffpfund)	44½
Industrial products		
Iron	Schippound (Schiffpfund)	163
White blankets	Piece	912
Chess	Piece	41
Rope yarn	Stones	92
Wooden plates	Sixty	40
Cloth	Box	1
Baggy cloth	Piece	130
Honey-cakes	Box	1
Fish		
Eels	Fass	24
Sturgeons	Achtel	.119

1 ring = 240 pieces

Notes

[1] A. Groth; *Statistik des Seehandels der Weichselhaffhäfen in den Jahren 1581-1712*, Ossolineum 1990, p. 10.

[2] Archiwum Panstwowe Gdansk (abbc, AP Gd.), 300, 19, Nr.16-18; Cz.Biernat: *Danziger Pfahlgeldbücher aus der zweiten Hälfte des 18.* Jahrhunderts sowie die Methode ihrer statistischen Bearbeitung, 'Pommerellenstudien' 1964.

[3] AP Gd., 369,1 Nr.2828-2830, 2832, 2833-2891.

[4] Geheimes Staatsarchiv Preußischen Kulturbesitzes Berlin, Ostpreußische Folianten, Nr.12887-12890, 12892-12893, 12896-12904, 12908, 12910-12912, 12915-12916, 12918, 12920-12986.

[5] A.E. Mierzwa: *England und Polen in der ersten Hälfte des 17.* Jahrhunderts, Warschau 1986, pp.65-66.

[6] J.K. Fedorowicz: *England's Baltic trade in the early seventeenth century.* A study of Anglo-Polish commercial diplomacy, Cambridge 1980, p. 175.

[7] Ibid. p. 73; vgl.: W.W. Boroszenko: *Handel und Kaufleute in Riga im 17.* Jahrhunderts, Riga 1985, pp. 136-137; Hinton, R.W.K.:*The Eastland Trade and the Commonweal in the Seventeenth Century*, Cambridge 1959.

[8] H. Zins: *England und die Baltik in der zweiten Hälfte des 16. Jahrhunderts. Der Ostseehandel englischer Kaufleute mit Polen in der elisabethanischen Epoche und die Eastland Company*, Wroclaw-Warschau-Krakau, 1967, p. 254.

[9] Ibid. p. 120.

English Merchants in Danzig

by

Walter Stark

I wish to complement the paper of Professor Groth by offering some observations about the connection between Danzig and England, especially between Danzig and Lynn, in the first half of the fifteenth century. Not a paper - only observations! I wish to highlight English references in the notebook of a Danzig merchant. In the Archiwum Pastwowe Gdansk is preserved the merchant-book of the Danzig merchant Johann Pisz with business notes from 1421 to 1456.[1] There are more than 200 names of merchants from Danzig, Poland, Lithuania, the Hanseatic towns of the Baltic, from the Netherlands and Scandinavia and also approximately 20 English names. This merchant-book is repeatedly used, but still unpublished.[2] What about the English in this book? They bring and sell salt, the so called 'baien solt' from the Atlantic coast, cloth from Colchester, Beverley and also 'lynen cloth' and canvas. The English bought and exported, at first, wax. Only once was the amount worth less than 100 Prussian marks (m.pr.); the other 9 transactions for wax were higher. For example: in 1438 a certain Jon Gylbert bought wax for 615 m.pr, and again in 1440 for 300 m.pr.[3] only from our merchant, Johann Pisz.

At this time several hundred merchants in Danzig wrote down in their books their trade and credit operations; generally every merchant used two or more books simultaneously. Of all these books from Danzig, only one is preserved. The facts contained in it present but a tiny sample of the total trade of this big port; nevertheless, they are all the more precious as they allow a limited insight into the real process of trading. In 1446 Jon Palynk bought wax and paid 530 m.pr.[4] Altogether, between 1431 to 1446, our Danzig merchant sold wax to English merchants to the value of 2,800 m.pr.

The second most important export was seal fat, bought for 751½ m.pr in total. After this the English purchased the so-called osmund, a brittle Swedish iron (brittle because its content was too high in carbon). As is generally known, Swedish iron export was largely directed to Lübeck. But in the middle decades of the 15th century the political climate in Lübeck for Englishmen was hostile and they therefore preferred to go for iron to Danzig. Altogether they bought 18½ lasts or 212 vats for 737 m.pr., and only from our Danzig merchant. The book records no transactions in timber and wood products such as ashes, pitch and tar. Our merchant does not seem to have offered these commodities for sale.

Finally, I wish to introduce to you a certain Richard Schottun. In Danzig in 1437 he bought wax and iron for 820 m.pr. Johann Pisz noted down in his book *'Ritzerd Schottun met her clawes roggen to hus'* (Richard Schotten met Mr Claus Rogge in his house) which means this host of Schottun belonged to the noblest society of the town i.e. the town councillors and court authority patricians.[5] Two years later, in 1439, Danzig replied to a Lynn complaint about the bad quality of timber by saying that it had a strict control system with three degrees of quality: 'good timber', 'wrak timber' and 'wrak-wrak timber'. But the foreign merchants mixed these degrees of timber quality, including the citizen of Lynn, Richard Schottun. Repeatedly he is said – *'mandatis se frivole opponens'* (boasting about ignoring regulations) – to have mixed good timber from Danzig with less good timber – *'que apud nos communi vocabulo wrak et wrak-wrak nuncupatur'* (what we call in colloquial language wrak and wrak wrak) - and at the same time to have maintained that all the timber came from Danzig.[6]

Schottun was well known in Danzig. Ten years before, in 1428, Richard Schottun, William Lochsmyth, also a Lynn man, and two other Englishmen, bought a vessel in Danzig, the hulk *Krystoffer*, for 1,600 m.pr. The money had to be paid by Whitsuntide, 1429, in Bruges in good English nobles.[7] (The exchange rate at this time was 1 noble = 3 m.pr.) It seems that the payment was delayed because in 1429 the Danzig merchant, Hans Mekelvelt, demanded 400 m.pr. from Richard Schottun in exchange for a quarter of a ship. The debtor was a certain Jon Wayen, one of the purchasers of the ship in the preceding year. Schottun gave the Danzig merchant, Diederich Moteler, as a guarantor who received from the same man 27½ Beverleysche cloths and 18 hundreds *'damdoke'* (?) as a deposit. The whole action ended in September 1429 with a compromise.[8] In the same year, 1429, Richard Schottun and Robert Loftus owed 598 m.pr. in Danzig. They promised to pay one half at Christmas and the other half at Easter the next year. Schottun promised not to leave Danzig earlier or to give a surety if he did so.[9]

I summarize: according to the Danzig sources a merchant from Lynn, Richard Schottun, had important trade relations with Danzig over ten years. He sold cloths, canvas and salt; he bought timber, wax, iron and a ship. He had business partners among the citizens of Danzig and lived in the house of a member of the city council and, last but not least, he had credit - in German: *'sinen loven'*!

This is an example of trading between England and Prussia in the first half of the fifteenth century - in spite of many difficulties and troubles.

Notes

[1] Archiwum Pastwowe Gdansk (AP Gd). Ksiega kupca Gdanskiego Jana Pisza. 300.R. F/4. (HB Pisz).

[2] v. Slaski, W., *Danziger Handel im XV.* Jahrhundert auf Grund eines . . . Handlungsbuches geschildert, phil Diss. Heidelberg 1905; Schmidt-Rimpler, W., *Geschichte des Kommissionsgeschäftes in Deutschland,* Bd. 1, Halle/S. 1915; Stark, W., *Untersuchungen zum Profit beim hansischen Handelskapital in der ersten Hälfte des 15.* Jahrhunderts, Weimar 1985, pp. 115-130.

[3] HB Pisz, fol. 93 r., 89 v.

[4] HB Pisz, fol. 85 r.

[5] HB Pisz, fol. 94 r.

[6] Hansisches Urkundenbuch, Bd. VII, 1, bearb, von H.G. v. Rundstedt, Weimar 1939, Nr. 474.

[7] AP Gd. Ksiega lawnicza od lat 1426-1438 (Book of the court of lay assessors 1426-1438), 300.43. la, fol 94 v. 1428 die Mauricii (1428 Sept. 22).

[8] AP Gd. 300. 43. 1a, fol. 122 v. 1429 feria Sexta post Jacobi (1429 July 29); fol. 126 v. 1429 feria secunda ante Michaelis (1429 Sept. 16).

[9] AP Gd. 300. 43, 1a, fol. 118 r., 1429 vig. Joh. bapt. (1429 Jun. 23).

FESTIVAL AND SPIRITUAL LIFE

The Beginnings of Public Dancing and Concerts in the Cities of the Hanseatic League

by

Walter Salmen

In 1607 in the Merchant Taylors' Hall in London there were, according to a description of the building, 'upon either side of the hall, in the windows near the upper end, galleries of seats, made for music'. The musicians who took their places on these elevated seats were visible to all the guests during the banqueting or dancing. Moreover, these seats effected a clearly visible separation between the guests and the minstrels serving them.

There were also 'scaffolds' or 'galleries' for musicians in other guild, town, drapers' and dance halls in England, as well as on the continent, from the Middle Ages. We ask: What were these used for? Who sat on them? What music was played from these balconies and on what occasions? This historical problem, and one also posed by numerous illustrations, opens one's eyes to the social and economic historical aspects connected to it, aspects that we shall look at in the exemplary cases of several localities belonging to the League of Hanseatic cities.

Did close relationships exist between the *'mercatores frequentantes sive menantes'*[1] and the *'joculatores'*? In other words, between two professions, the majority of whose practitioners were obliged to lead a life on the road or on the water, in some cases to undertake long journeys, to be constantly confronted with the unfamiliar. The one lived ambulant as a travelling merchant, the other as an itinerant minstrel. The one dealt, as trader, in material goods and accumulated property and riches, the other transported dances, songs, stories and news, frequently from far away, and usually remained poor. Both had need of one another on journeys: for entertainment in return for payment, for acoustical representation in the market towns, for the celebration of feasts and, as compensation for the life of business and work, for pastime. In addition, minstrels were employed at the market places to attract customers with their pipes and tabors. Organized in guilds, the merchants contributed significantly, as sponsors, to the improvement of the standard of living of the minstrels, who were for the most part socially ostracized.

The beginnings of public dancing in dance halls

In medieval society rounds and dances were more than just an entertainment with emphasis on pleasure. On the contrary, it was something that permeated all aspects of life and social affiliations and something that only a few (monks, for example) could avoid. Dancing was generally regarded as one of the fundamental social graces. It was considered an indication of the position that one could achieve in the hierarchy, of social advancement and acceptance, but also of social decline. One danced everywhere: in the churches, in the cemeteries, at public as well as private legal proceedings, and at political meetings.[2] Someone who belonged to the aristocracy or the patrician class had to exercise this privilege at all times at these exclusive events. For these events to take place in suitable surroundings, princes had banqueting halls built into their castles, halls of such dimensions that a specific choreography could be realized in them. The merchant aristocracy in the self-governing cities, in emulation of the nobility, fitted out guild, town, or even specially built dance halls for the same purpose. Thus, there was, for example, from the middle of the 13th century in Dortmund, a town hall with a banqueting hall on the first floor that was more than thirty metres in length. From then until well into the 17th century, thirty metres was considered to be the standard measure. The same can be ascertained from the great hall, the so-called 'Dornse', in the old town hall in Brunswick, at least from the end of the 14th century. So, too, in Bremen where, in 1430, after a court hearing 'auff dem Rathause', so-called 'Nachttentze' were held. Let us take a more detailed look, on the basis of four Hanseatic cities, at these prestige-lending investments in banqueting and dance halls made by the municipalities or by the guilds.

Cologne. In Cologne there was a 'domus in quam cives conveniunt' or house of citizens mentioned around 1135. In 1149 it was called 'domus civium inter Judeos sita'. The reference 'inter Judeos' contained in this description is especially noteworthy because in the 12th century the wealthy Jewish community also owned, across from this town hall, a 'domus universitatis iudeorum', which in 1288 is more clearly described as 'speylhuz' (a dance or playhouse).[3] This meeting house, primarily intended to be a wedding or bridal house, was indeed the oldest in Europe. Presumably, it also served as the model for those buildings erected in the following period for Cologne's Christian citizens to dance in. Already in the year 1231 there existed here a 'platea joculatorum' (a place where players or minstrels lived), later called 'spilmansgazze', one of this profession's oldest urban settlements.[4] This also deserves mention in the present context because minstrels were needed to provide professional festive and dance music in the old town hall's 'Langer

**Fig. 1 The Gürzenich in Cologne - east view, built before 1447.
A watercolour of 1855 by Jakob Hinden.** *(Cologne Stadtmuseum, Graphics
Collection).*

Saal', known since the 14th century, with its pointed-arch, tunnel-vaulted
ceiling. Renamed *'Hanseatischer Saal'* in the 18th century, this room for
festivities, banquets and dances was - making its purpose clear -
metaphorically decorated with paintings of a flautist, a drummer and a
bagpipes player, among others.[5] The hall was rectangular and long (28.70 x
7.25 x 9.70 metres), and thus satisfied etiquette and was suitable for the
refined choreographies of the pavane, or slow dance.

The economic prosperity of Cologne made it possible for a separate
municipal banqueting and dance hall, the Gürzenich, (Fig.1) to be built
between 1437 and 1444, for no less than eighty thousand gold florins. In this
building, which in times of declining business was also used as a market hall,
there were spacious halls on both floors. The room on the top floor had
dimensions (54.67 x 23.85 x 19.50 metres) that were unique in the 15th
century. This room size surpassed even that of dance halls in the castles of
the kings. For heating in winter, there were two stone fireplaces with friezes
showing minstrels, a dance as well as a mummery.[6](Fig.2). It is known that
emperors and princes, merchants and artisans, all came to dance in the
Gürzenich.

Fig. 2 Relief over fireplace depicting 'merrymakers mocking a clown' in the Great Hall of the Gürzenich - destroyed in World War Two.
(Cologne, Rheinisches Bildarchiv, Photograph RBA no. 17198).

Since this double offering of dance halls was obviously not able to meet the demand, Cologne's city council treated itself to a third house with a dance hall, namely the building across from the Gürzenich at Quatermarkt Nos.1-3, which had already been leased as a *'Bruloftshaus'* or wedding house around 1400. This house was bought by the council in 1561, remodelled and enlarged. Thus, on the threshold of the modern era, the Cologne populace had four impressive dance halls at its disposal, each measuring over two hundred square metres, outdoing even the imperial cities of Southern Germany.

Lübeck afforded itself a town hall, enlarged in a number of stages from the early 14th century onwards, which also featured a 'Hansasaal'. Besides rooms for the market, for town council meetings and public assemblies, there was on the first floor, even before 1400, a hall of about thirty metres in length, without any sight-obstructing pillars, which had been added on to the south side of the *'Burgersaal'*. This was called the *'Danzelhus'*.[7] (Fig.3). Here too, as in Cologne, the room capacity was apparently not great enough, for between 1442 and 1444, this dance house was extended by a building that contained open halls for commerce downstairs and a further large ban-

70

Fig. 3 City Hall in Lübeck (before 1939). The dance hall is in the part of the building on the right of the picture.

queting hall upstairs. In this imposing town hall, integrating three hall buildings in a uniquely concentrated construction programme, the most important aspects of a city government were accommodated: administration, commerce (drapers' hall), and organised festivity (dance hall). The many decrees issued at Lübeck concerning leisure activities included the dances held here, with restrictive regulations limiting the employment of *'spilluden'* (since 1316 there had been a *'comes joculatorum'* or head of the musicians), of the Stadtmusikanten, who were first mentioned in documents in 1343, and also of the Ratsmusikanten, who had been granted their first statutes in 1404. All these musicians served not only the council but also the *'koplude kumpanye'*, or merchants' association called the *Zirkelgesellschaft*, the *Bergenfahrern* and other groups. These guilds repeatedly engaged the minstrels for their banquets in the *Schütting* or in city palaces in which, since the 14th century, there were large, four to five metres high *'Dielen'* and later also annexes built in the courtyards. These too were used as dance halls.[8]

Lüneburg. In this North German city, which was incorporated into the Hansa in 1371, a privileged gentry established itself from the 13th century. Owing to a lucrative salt monopoly, the holders of refinery licences, the *'Sülfmeister'* (masters of the salt works), were able to qualify for election to the council and to form a patrician class. Within the duchy of Brunswick-Lüneburg, this city, independent until 1639, occupied a special position which, on the basis of the wealth accumulated during the 15th and 16th

Fig. 4 Lüneburg: The Fürstensaal (Princes Hall) in the Town Hall (as it is today).

centuries, gave rise to a proud, civic self-assurance. In the context of the history of dance, this manifested itself in the erection and furnishing of several banqueting halls, including those belonging to the city council and in the homes of several wealthy patricians.

About 1300, the city council built a two-storey *'domus pannicidae'*, a drapers' hall, a free-standing edifice next to the first town hall of about 1230. It was a brick hall building, the lower floor of which served the clothiers as a salesroom, and with a wine cellar beneath. With the increasing prosperity of the *'Sülfmeister'* and the heightened self-confidence of the city councillors, the demand became greater in the 15th century for a larger and, above all, wider hall for dancing. Consequently, work began in 1449 with the renovation of the so-called *'Fürstensaal'*, the *'danzhus'*, which is extant today. (Figs. 4 and 5). This banqueting hall of about 318 square metres was 27.66 metres long and an average of 11.50 metres wide.[9] This expanse, which was not broken up by columns or pillars, was covered with Flemish tiles. Fireplaces on the west and east sides made it possible to hold dances in winter too. Benches were placed along the walls for the spectators, and five Gothic chandeliers provided for radiant illumination of the festivities. In 1535, on the occasion of a *'Hansetag'* (an occasional meeting of the towns of the Hanseatic League), portraits of the dukes and duchesses of Brunswick-Lüneburg were painted on canvases above the oak panelling. For this reason, the room was henceforth no longer called *'danzhus'* but rather *'Fürstensaal'*. A kitchen connected to the banqueting hall provided refreshments for the hosts as well as for the guests.[10]

Many of the *'Hansetage'* held in close succession between 1412 and 1619 in Lüneburg found their social high point in this banqueting hall. The many licensed minstrels, recorded in the Lüneburg council's official archives, who came from other towns in the Hanseatic League, contributed musically to the festivities, as did the *'figellatori'* and the *'pipere und trumpere des Rades to luneborgh'* (pipers and trumpeters of the Lüneburg town council). The former are recorded from about 1335, the latter from about 1430. In 1443 there were five Ratsmusiker, from 1546 seven, of which three were *'Spellude'* (wind players), three *'Gigerden'* (string players), and one a lutanist.[11] Due to several subsequent building alterations, it can no longer be determined where they were positioned in the dance hall of the *'Gewandhaus'* or cloth hall.

Fig. 5 The Danzhus (Low German Dance House). Today the Heinrich Heine Haus, Am Ochsenmarkt 1 (c.1563). Registrar Office; the ceiling painting is the original. *(Photograph in private possession).*

73

Of course, the Lüneburg Ratsmusiker did not just provide the music for dancing in the *Fürstensaal*, but also *'auf dem Schützen'*, that is, in the meeting house of the merchants or *'Schütting'*; for example, for the famous *'Kopefahrt'* of the *'Sülfmeister'*, a carnival event. Some of these rich patricians additionally engaged the minstrels in their own homes. Among these, the house of Hartwig Witzendorff, situated at Ochsenmarkt No.1, next to the town hall, attracts special attention even today. In 1563, this *'Sülfmeister'* erected an impressive complex of buildings. It consisted of a typical house with an adjoining and painted *'danzhus'* of about sixty-five square metres, today known as the Heine House, and housing the registry office. Beside this, there was a residential range (today housing the Volksbank), stables and market stalls.[12]   In this two-storey, gable-fronted oblong hall building *(giebelständigen Längsdielenhaus)* with a *'Diele'* suitable for dancing, and an encircling balustrade, splendid balls attended by princes were held; for example, in 1599 on the occasion of the *'Kopefahren'*. What might have taken place then was captured in 1599 by Anton Möller, in a painting from Danzig, depicting an elegant dance that was similarly held in the *'Diele'* of a patrician house.[13]   Dance music from the 16th century has not been preserved. A Franciscus Witzendorff Lünaeb did, however, leave behind a keyboard tablature, compiled between 1655 and 1659, containing dances, songs, chorales and preludes, among which would be found some of the pieces performed at dances in the house of this patrician family.[14]

Danzig. In Danzig the interests of the citizens in terms of dancing and festivities were satisfied differently from those in the three Hansa cities observed so far. Here the town hall was exclusively the home of the administration, the judiciary and politics. For all that, a gallery for musicians was also fitted into this building. The merchants, however, celebrated weddings and dances in the guild halls, in the Artushof on the Langer Markt as well as in the Georgshalle on Langgasse.[15]

The Artushof was first mentioned in 1350, its owner being given as the *'Compagny'* of the *'gemeine Kaufmann'*. From 1450 this public building was the seat of the merchants' association, which was a very exclusive body. Following a fire, the Artushof was rebuilt in 1481 with a larger, three-span hall. Here the guilds held their banquets with *'Spellüden Inn der Köre'* (minstrels in the lofts) on the occasion of the annual election of the *'Aelterleute'* (masters of the guilds).[16] These pipers and trumpeters played at such events from 1400 if not before. Employed in pairs (a pair each of pipers and trumpeters), they were called *'Havepiper'*. The Danzig Ratspfeifer were recruited after 1500 from this ensemble belonging to the guilds. They were still required to play at least once a week in the Artushof.

The St George Confraternity maintained a club house from 1494 for its own festivities.

A look at other towns

To complete this sketch of public dance halls in four cities, this section looks at activities in some other towns of the Hanseatic League. In Reval, as in Danzig, for example, were the *'groten gildestauen'* (guild charter meetings), the banquet of St Olav's guild or *'der knuthen off Sunte oleffs gilden'*, the places for splendid *'bruthkosten'* (wedding banquets) with typical *'grote spele'* (large wind formations) and *'denßen'*.[17] In the most important Flemish Hansa trading post, Bruges, on the other hand, one danced in the town hall in the 15th century, in the reception hall known as the *'burg'*.[18] This room at one time had a balcony for the musicians, a so-called *'paradisekin'*, built into it. In addition, 'mummeries' financed by the town took place in the palace. In Antwerp, the *'Oosters Huis'* of the German merchants was one of the social centres of cultivated conviviality. Here, musical instruments from Lübeck were used, some of which are preserved to this day in the Musée d'Instruments in Brussels.

The beginnings of public concerts

In dancing and music-making, amateurs as well as professionals play an active role in musical life. Listening to performances, on the other hand, is indicative of passive participation. The latter is especially so in everyday life today. Media transmissions of music of every sort from all parts of the world are countless. The institutions required for this were already present in some cities of antiquity. The associated marketing system disappeared during the early Middle Ages as did the idea, which had had once inspired concerts in antiquity. In the 14th century, it was initially the Hansa towns that again organized the performance of music as a publicly funded com-munal service. How can we explain this initiative?

Only growing and prospering towns could afford to free music-making from its traditional religious and other constraints and allow it to become an aesthetic performance simply offered *'ad gaudium'*. This could, at its best, become pure art. Out of 'courtly pretension' (*hofieren*) developed auto-nomous, entertaining performance. A prerequisite for this was the training and engagement of specialists. This began in the 13th century with the introduction of *'waites et trompeurs'* into the urban life of Wismar, Lübeck, Rostock, Bruges, Antwerp, Lüneburg, and other towns after 1270. These civic minstrels were *'servans de la ville'* or *'piper van de stad'*. In addition, after 1300, further *'histriones ville'* (Bruges 1297) or *'menistreuls van der stede'*

(Bruges 1368/69), who struck, blew, bowed or plucked various instruments, became established.[19]

Besides these Stadt and Ratsmusikanten, starting in the 15th century there were also minstrels in the service of confraternities, the so-called 'Gildespielleute' or 'Rollmusikanten'. In the churches, organ-playing clergy and monks were replaced by professional lay organists. With the advent of professional musicians, who were contractually protected and resident, secular music, free of ritual, could be performed on Sundays and holidays.

The earliest evidence for this is provided by the city of Wismar on the Baltic Sea. Here, a regulation was laid down for an organized municipal ensemble. It stipulated: 'Item joculatores hic in Ciuivate jacere solentes quibus premissa datur libertas debent singulis diebus dominicis et festivis infra festa pasche et johannis quando domi fuerint Ciuibus nostris in Reseto de vespere seruire et ludes suos exercere'. Which means: In return for the privileges granted them, the minstrels were to play free of charge, for the enjoyment of the citizens, on summer evenings in the Rosengarten, one of the town's pleasure gardens. This may have been something like the Sunday band concerts that are given even today in municipal parks. The beginnings of subsidized public concerts are certainly to be found here.[20]

After Wismar, we come to Bruges. From the 14th century, in order to preserve the sympathies of its rulers and foreign merchants in view of the gloomy economic background, when the market square was filled with buyers and sellers, the crowd was inspired to do business by music from the belfry or from the corner of the old town hall. A special stage for the minstrels was built onto this old town hall in 1466/67. The purpose of this public performance was thus to encourage buying and selling, just as today the customers of department stores and supermarkets are bombarded with sound over loudspeakers.

In 1480 a further step was taken. The city of Bruges agreed to pay if the four to five 'tubicines et mimi hujus opidi Brugensis' pledged to play, after the 'laudes Beate Marie', the 'lof' (a Marian service) or 'Salve' in the Church of St Donatian, every day during the May Fair. This means that they were to give, without charging an entrance fee, and outside a liturgical context, 'Salve concerts' after compline, with polyphonic motets composed especially for this specific purpose. With this, the administration of the town once again took on the responsibility to provide entertainment for the citizens and the important market visitors, and also to demonstrate both the professional status and social standing of the town musicians. In addition to these public concerts, the confraternities also organized for the first time 'real subscription concerts' in the guild-houses.[21]

This example from Bruges can be supplemented by others. In Kampen, around 1474, the city players were to 'play the lof in front of the City Hall', thus to play outdoors; in Utrecht in 1489, they were to perform in the Buerkerk. When Maximilian I visited Bruges to confirm its municipal privileges, the city musicians played *Ave regina celorum* followed by *'liedekens van muzyck'* on the town square, that is to say, secular pieces for entertainment. This practice, supportive of both mercantile and political interests, was continued later in many other towns. In 1714, for example, the city of Norwich arranged for the waites to perform monthly 'musick meetings for the accommodation and diversion of the lovers of musick in this city'. In Danzig's Artushof there were similar twice weekly offerings.

The organists were also enlisted as soloists in these performances. In Utrecht in 1581, the canons of St Marie instructed their organist that from 1583 he was to play the organ on all normal chapter-days and additionally on every Sunday, Tuesday and Friday, as well as on the Apostle and Marian days from eleven to twelve o'clock. In 1593, in Leiden, the organist Cornelius Schuyt received his contract as a municipal employee with the stipulation that he 'play on the city's organ in the church ... for the recreation and pleasure of the parishioners and, through this playing, keep them out of the inns and taverns, this is to take place every day following the evening prayer ... and each time for an hour'. This contractual arrangement certainly marks the beginning, in Leiden, of organ concerts independent of the liturgical rites. For the parishioners this meant that they had to accept the church musician, who had previously served exclusively in the divine service, in the role of the soloist playing for secular edification and entertainment too.

The influence of Calvinism in Holland and England with the complete removal of the organ from the actual church service, together with its use as an instrument for concert music outside church services, encouraged free organ music, especially the fantasia. Since the Calvinist church did not offer the organist a place, he was often engaged by the town and thus found himself in the role of the town musician.

The sensation that these organ concerts caused in Holland, and their artistic importance beyond the borders of the towns, was so great that, in the opinion of art historian William S. Heckscher, there was only a single cultural event in the Netherlands of that time with which they could be compared: the annual event that took place in Amsterdam in the form of theatrical performances. The assumption is certainly justified that these concerts in the Netherlands were based on a long-standing tradition, in which the churches were converted, after the vesper service *(Abendlob)* on market or parish fair days, into 'communication centres', whereby, as documented, the organist for St Bavo's in Haarlem, was required to supply the music.

The international dissemination of the Dutch organ concert tradition which, by the way, also had counterparts in England, can be observed in the Baltic Sea area in the 16th century. An impressive growth in Dutch influence in many towns on the south coast of the North and Baltic Seas about 1600, resulted from the expulsion of Protestants from the southern Netherlands by the Spanish. The reputation of Sweelinck, the Amsterdam organ master, spread, as shown by the list compiled by G. Gerdes of his known pupils, to central Germany (the Scheidt brothers, Anders Düben) and Berlin (Aug. Brücke). By far the greatest number of pupils, however, came from the port towns on the North and Baltic Seas, where the region north of the Elbe is well represented by five organists (Jac. Praetorius II, Joh. Praetorius, Scheidemann, U. Cernitz and Petrus Hasse). This region was also apparently operating as a sort of clearing house with Sweelinck pupils dispatched to Scandinavia (A. Düben to Stockholm, and J. Lorentz to Copenhagen).[22]

The famous 'Abendspielen' (evening concerts) of organist Franz Tunder in Lübeck, starting in 1641, also belong to this tradition. Beginning in 1673, Dietrich Buxtehude gave his concerts, which he called 'Abendmusiken', for the 'Commercirende Zünfte' (commercial guilds) at St Mary's in the same city. Even when these 'Abendspielen' took place in churches, we should not assume that the audience's conduct was as disciplined as it is today at a symphony orchestra concert. On the contrary, from the Netherlands to Danzig it was reported that these organ concerts were 'pleasurable', and that the churchgoers played cards and drank wine. Constantin Huygens, a diplomat and musician, observed in 1640 that 'singles' went to these concerts for amorous purposes; the 'non-singles', on the other hand, attempted to make use of these social meetings for business.

Let us now go back to the beginning when we asked the question: What purpose would these 'galleries of seats, made for music' have served? It is now clear that such facilities were for high-society dancing and concerts, which contributed to public leisure and entertainment in some towns on the continent.

Notes

[1] See Klaus Friedland, Die Hanse (Stuttgart, 1991), p. 31 ff.

[2] See Walter Salmen, *Dance and Dancing in the Middle Ages and Renaissance* (London, forthcoming).

[3] Walter Salmen, 'Der Juden Tanzhaus' im Mittelalter', *Freiburger Rundbrief, Zeitschrift für christlich-jüdische Begegnung* NF 2 (1997): 94 ff.

[4] H. Keusen, *Topographie der Stadt Cöln im Mittelalter* (Bonn, 1910), II, 36 ff, 229.

[5] *Die Kunstdenkmäler der Stadt Köln,* ed. Paul Clemen (Düsseldorf, 1930), II,4, p.215 ff and fig. 146; Fried Mühlberg, 'Der Hansasaal des Kölner Rathauses', *Wallraf-Richartz-Jahrbuch* 36 (1974), p. 65 ff.

[6] H. Keusen, *Topographie der Stadt Cöln im Mittelalter* (Bonn, 1910), II, 36*ff*, 229.

[7] *Die Kunstdenkmäler der Stadt Köln,* ed. Paul Clemen (Düsseldorf, 1930), II,4, p.215*ff* and fig. 146; Fried Mühlberg, 'Der Hansasaal des Kölner Rathauses', *Wallraf-Richartz-Jahrbuch* 36 (1974), p. 65*ff.*

[8] Ibid., p. 278*ff.*

[9] *Die Kunstdenkmäler der Provinz Hannover,* ed. Carl Wolff (Hannover, 1906), III, 2-3, p. 247*ff.*, 354*ff.*

[10] See Stephan Albrecht, 'Beobachtung zu Baugeschichte des Lüneburger Rathauses', in *'Alles was Recht ist': 750 Jahre Stadtrecht in Lüneburg,* exhibition catalogue 1997, p. 46*ff.*

[11] Walter Salmen, *Der Spielmann im Mittelalter* (Innsbruck, 1983); Horst Walter, *Musikgeschichte der Stadt Lüneburg* (Tutzing, 1967), p. 21*ff.*

[12] Gernot Fischer, 'Das Heine-Haus Am Ochsenmarkt 1 in Lüneburg', in *Berichte zur Denkmalpflege in Niedersachsen* 11 (1991), p. 94*ff.*; Werner Preuß, *Das Heinrich Heine Haus in Lüneburg* (Lüneburg, 1994).

[13] Gabriele and Walter Salmen, *Bilder zur Musikgeschichte in Ostmitteleuropa,* Musik des Ostens 13 (Kassel, 1992) table 62/1.

[14] Walter, *Musikgeschichte der Stadt Lüneburg,* p. 135.

[15] Erich Leyser, *Die Baugeschichte der Stadt Danzig* (Cologne and Vienna, 1992), p. 143*ff.*

[16] Hermann Rauschning, *Geschichte der Musik und Musikpflege in Danzig* (Danzig, 1931), p. 22.

[17] Hans Joachim Moser, 'Zur mittelalterlichen Musikgeschichte der Stadt Coln', *Archiv fur Musikwissenschaft* 1 (1918/19); 139*f*.

[18] Reinnard Strohm, *Music in Late Medieval Bruges* (Oxford, 1990), p. 82.

[19] Heinrich W. Schwab, *Die Anfänge des weltlichen Berufsmusikertums in der mittelalterlichen Stadt* (Kassel, 1982).

[20] Walter Salmen, *Das Konzert,* (Munich, 1988), p. 12*ff.*

[21] Strohm, *Music in Late Medieval Bruges,* p. 83.

[22] Arnfried Edler, *Der Nordelbishe Organist,* (Kassel, 1982), p. 47*f.*

Fig. 1 Boston, Parish Church of St Botolph's ('The Stump'), tomb slab
of Wissel Smalenburg, † 1312 Sept. 15.

Church and Church Business in Hanseatic Agencies

by

Klaus Krüger

Only a few miles away from here, in the Greyfriars monastery of Boston, there is the memorial slab of the merchant Wissel Smalenburg (Fig. 1). This slab dates back to the first quarter of the 14th century.[1] The deceased is portrayed in frontal posture at the middle field of the slab praying with open eyes under an architectural canopy, which symbolizes the heavenly Jerusalem. A dog is lying at his feet. The circumscription is in Latin in nice round capital letters and acknowledges:

Hic iacet Wisselus dictus Smalenburgh, civis et mercator Monasteriensis, qui obiit feria sexta post nativitatem beate Marie virginis anno domini Millesimo trecentesimo duodecimo. Anima eius requiescat in pace, amen.

Here lies Wissel called Smalenburg, citizen and merchant of Münster, who died AD 1312 on 15 September. May his soul rest in peace. Amen.

This inscription and the tombstone itself, a hard blue-grey limestone probably of Belgian origin, draw attention to the fact that the monument has been imported from the continent. Comparable pieces can be found at Sudbury (Suffolk) and Brading (Isle of Wight), at Hastings and Playden (Sussex).[2] So this is not a sole example. In Boston we encounter a German merchant from the Westphalian area who certainly did trade with merchants of the English east coast. He was so well integrated there that, after his death, his mortal remains were not taken back to his home country but a monument of the highest artistic standards was ordered from the area of the River Maas and transported to Boston. The organisation and cost of that must have been immense.

Unfortunately, the monument itself does not give further information about the deceased. However, the foot-rests of some slabs of native provenance from the 15th century help to identify the business in which the particular merchant was involved:[3] a wine trader in Cirencester, whose name is unknown, has a cask at his feet (Fig. 2), a certain John Lyndewode the younger from Linwood (Lincolnshire), who died in 1421, has a pack of wool at his feet on which even his own house-brand can be identified (Fig. 3). The same applies to the monument of an unnamed wool trader from Northleach (Gloucestershire) who died in 1485 (Fig. 4). Apart from the pack of wool, there is a recognizable sheep on his slab, which confirms the content of the pack. In contrast to this, our Hanseatic merchant in Boston stands completely in the tradition of the noble monument where the dog is

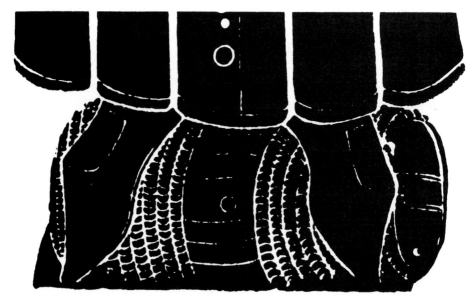

Fig. 2 Cirencester (Gloucestershire), slab of an unknown wine trader, c.1400.

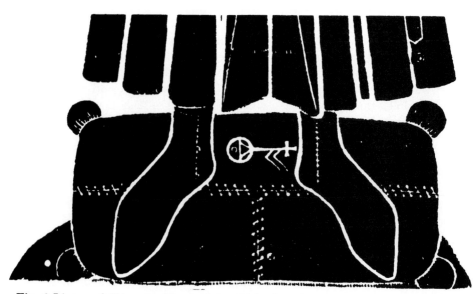

Fig. 3 Linwood (Lincolnshire), slab of John Lyndewode the Younger, † 1421.

regarded as a symbol of social status as well as a religious symbol.[4] Here we have to ask if a merchant of the Hanseatic League had to have ready two or more memorials, since he would not know where he would die (or be buried).[5] Wissel Smalenburg wanted to be buried in Boston at the Greyfriars like many of his Hanseatic companions.

Fig. 4 Northleach (Gloucestershire), slab of an unknown wool trader, † 1485.

What kind of relations did the Hanseatic League maintain, through its agencies and factories, with the church and its representatives? Two possibilities can be considered. First, the religious conditions and life of the hometown or towns were adopted by the particular agency and imitated. According to this possibility, the church of the Holy Virgin at Bergen could be regarded as a copy of the church with the identical name in Lübeck from where the majority of the *Bergenfahrer* came. Second, every agency developed its own social and charitable institutions, which are the basis of a growing self-confidence abroad. Bruges could be considered as a prototype in which a close interconnection of citizens, clergy and religious com-munities can be identified.

Bruges

The present research focussed mainly on the links between the Hanseatic community in Bruges and local religious institutions, and the Carmelite monastery where the Hanse had its headquarters. Other religious institutions as well as individuals also play a significant role, as will be shown.[6]

Decisive for the religious relations of the Hanseatic merchants in Bruges is the often quoted fact that there did not exist a separate district inside the town in which Hanseatic people could live and hold their assemblies. In the second half of the 13th century, when the German Hanse began to establish itself in Bruges, it had to adapt to the circumstances existing after the plan to found a new colony of merchants in Damme had failed. Thus the merchants lived in various houses and inns scattered through the town.[7] Occasionally, there is also evidence of Hanseatic property. There was some concentration of Germans in the north-east of the town near the Carmelite monastery, which became increasingly important to the Hanseatic League, and was near the Easterlings' place, an area named after the merchants. In 1457, the town council allowed the Germans to control this neighbourhood. Here, the Germans owned seven houses which they had received from the chapter of the church of Our Lady St Mary.[8] After their return from Utrecht in 1457, the Hanseatic merchants owned a house which was magnificently extended in 1478. This house was one of the most imposing buildings in the whole town and it kept its importance through being the main meeting place of the German merchants. Owning property brought about closer integration of merchants into the town, especially when they married native women. This did not cause a change in their property rights.[9]

The privileges of 1309 and 1360 granted the free choice of burial place to the Hanseatic merchants: '*Voort moghen de coopmanne vorseid hare sepulturen kiesen, waer dat zii willen, behouden der prochian recht, daer zii in sterven*' (Furthermore the named merchants may choose their burial where they wish to, reserving the rights of the parish where they die.)[10] So, on the one hand, it was everyone's personal decision in which church or monastery he would be buried and where he wanted the commemorative ceremonies to be held. On the other hand, this right was limited in favour of the relevant parish, although this did not mean that a parochial constraint existed. Compared to Lübeck, for instance, there is nothing known about a conflict between single churches and monasteries of the mendicant orders in Bruges. Renée Rößner demonstrated this with his study of the relations of the Hanseatic merchants with the mendicant monasteries in Bruges.[11]

At the Augustinians' priory, the German merchants owned five graves according to a document of the monks from 1459.[12] They were free to decide who should be buried there but the parish in which the person affected had died had a right to a share in decisions. The parishes in which the different monasteries were situated also exerted an influence in the matter of funerals. Already in 1286 the Augustinian monks and the chapter of St Mary's had come to an agreement about the erection of the monastery church. According to this, St Mary's was entitled to control funerals.

In the case of the Dominicans, similar circumstances can be recognized. The monastery of the predicants was founded in 1234 on the orders of Joan, Countess of Flanders. The friars of the Dominican order were obligated to the chapter of St Donatian and to the parish of the Holy Cross to which the monastery belonged; the monks were liable to pay taxes to them. The funeral ceremonies of persons who intended to be buried at the Dominicans had first to take place at Holy Cross. Both events are connected with the founding of this particular monastery; settlements of compensation were concluded with the parish that had transferred its parochial rights to the newly founded monastery. Evidence of burials of foreign merchants can be found in all the four mendicant orders in Bruges.

In Bruges, as in all the other Hanseatic agencies, the eldermen more or less held the position that the councils held in the home towns. In the presence of the eldermen a merchant's last will could be written.[13] The German agency in Bruges acted as the administrator of the property of the deceased Hanseatic merchant. So heirs and their authorized representatives frequently turned to the German agency in Bruges requesting the handing over of bequeathed property. The death of a member of the community affected all merchants. There exists a document from 1375 according to which the death of a member of the community had to be announced in all inns and houses of Hanseatic merchants by the *clerck off cnape*. It was the duty of all Hanseatic merchants to gather at the place of their companion's death and to be present at the funeral ceremonies in the church, otherwise they were fined: *de sal hebben verbuert drie grote also dicke, alse he dit versumede* (those who failed to attend, to be fined three grotes every time).[14] The money collected in this way was to contribute to the funeral ceremonies. Furthermore, the regular authorised services of the community were fully integrated in religious ceremonies and the remem-brance of the deceased. We can find out more about the religious life of the community from the so-called *Leitfaden*, the 'manual of the eldermen of the German agency in Bruges', which was written about 1500, and certainly gives an account of earlier conditions.[15]

Among the four great mendicant orders, which were resident in Bruges, the monastery of the Carmelite friars occupied an outstanding position.[16] The German merchants used the monastery church and the refectory for their gatherings and for meetings with other merchants. Especially, the elections of the eldermen and the religious ceremonies associated with these elections took place here. The secular importance which the monastery had for the German Hanse is underlined by the fact that the representatives of the Hanse and the English entrusted the documents of the peace treaty of Utrecht, which were locked up in a wooden coffer, to the prior of the Carmelites, Cornelius de Wise in 1475.[17] When in 1447/48 representatives

85

of the Hanseatic towns and of the four *Leden* of Flanders came together for negotiations about the privileges of the Hanse in Bruges, a mass of the Holy Spirit was said in the church of the monastery, *up dat unse lieve here God dersulver heren bodeschap und werve int beste und tot enen gueden eynde voeghen wolde, welke misse costede 14 schillings 10 grossi* (so as to pray to God to bring about a good end to the meeting of those our lords which mass made 14 schillings 10 grossi.). [18]

Although we are not told about the origins of the relations between the Hanseatic merchants and the Carmelite friars, German merchants had been involved with them since 1263, according to the 32nd chapter of the *Leitfaden*.[19] The religious ceremonies which accompanied the annual election of the merchant council in the refectory, and the reading of the privileges, are thoroughly described in the manual. On the day before the election, a Saturday, the *clercs* had to inform the community about the gathering at the Carmelites.[20] On Sunday, a mass dedicated to the Holy Spirit took place, accompanied by the playing of the organ and the whole choir. In the mass, the red ornaments *(roden ornamente)* of the merchants and the instruments of the Eucharist, which the merchants owned, were used: the chalice, the mass-pots of silver, the censer and the *osculatorium*.[21] The exact amount of money to be paid to the clergyman at mass is mentioned in the 12th chapter of the *Leitfaden*. The value of each individual candle is noted as well. Secretaries and servants of the merchant community were trusted to make sure that greenery was scattered all over the floor of the church and to drape wall-hangings with the portraits of the Emperor and the seven electors in the high choir.[22] The political significance of that demonstration manifests itself, regardless of the difficult relations between the Hanse and the Empire. After the mass, the election and swearing in of the eldermen and jurors took place in the refectory. In the afternoon, shortly before the transfer of office, the old and the newly elected eldermen met for a formal banquet.[23] One week later, a mass dedicated to the Holy Trinity was said. It preceded a reading of the council's privileges and the statutes and ordinances of the merchant community.[24] A banquet and a renewed reading of the privileges in the presence of all the merchants followed. On the following Monday, a requiem mass was celebrated in which all the merchants were obliged to take part. The mass was dedicated to all merchants who had died at sea and on Hanseatic duty.[25] In the middle of the choir a catafalque was erected which was covered with the pall of the merchant; the church was decorated with the black paraments of the community. At this requiem mass, a sum of money was given to the poor in general, *(armen int ghemene)*. A resolution, agreed in August 1485 by the merchant community, was the basis of the ceremony.[26] Furthermore, it was agreed to celebrate a mass of the Holy Spirit in remembrance of the return of the merchants from Utrecht to Bruges in 1457. This was to take place annually on the day after the day of St Laurentius' day, which is the 11th of August, in the monastery of the Carmelites. It was also agreed that the shrine with the weights and measures and the archives of the merchant community be kept at the Carmelites. The clerks of the agency had the responsibility for the deceased merchant's writings, trade books and *cleynode* (perhaps relics?).[27]

Chapters 31 and 32 regulate the charitable work of the Hanseatic agency. Every year in the middle of winter (around Christmas) as well as on Good Friday, alms had to be given to the four mendicant orders, to the sick in the hospitals and to different kinds of poor and prisoners. The Carmelites themselves, the clerks of the *camer van Brugge*, the harbour officers, the servants of the sovereign, all received gifts and others besides.

But there were connections to the other mendicant orders too: to the Dominicans, Franciscans and Augustinians. The German merchants donated glass windows for their monasteries upon which the arms of the Emperor and the seven electors were depicted.[28] The relationship with the Augustinians was especially close. In 1375, Prussian traders donated antiphonies and prayers here; prior and convent committed themselves to celebrate the ceremonies weekly and to pay a fine to the Carmelite monastery if they omitted the celebration.[29] The Prussians are called benefactors of the monastery, *qui nostro predicto conventu in diversis beneficiis multa bona diversimode fecerunt* (who did so much good in different ways for the said monastery). Apart from the Carmelites, the Augustinians are the only other order in which funerals of Hanseatic merchants can be found. In 1459 the monks guaranteed five graves to the Hanse, though they must have been occupied since the 14th century.[30] Two of the graves were situated in the choir and covered with brass plates. The others were in front of the chapel of St Barbara.

A close relationship existed with some parish churches, particularly St Mary's, St Salvator, St Jacob and St Gillis.[31] At the end of the 15th century the Hanseatic community supplied them with glass windows too, each having the picture of the Emperor and the seven electors on them. In this connection, the manual refers to the lost book of the merchants in which had been listed all the donations. The Easterlings also took part in the maintenance of some of the parish churches of Bruges, especially of their glass windows: St James, St Gillis, St Salvator, St Mary's, St Magdalene's (formerly St Catherine's), St Anne's, St Walpurga, St Donatian.[32]

Some merchants wished to be and were buried in the parish churches of Bruges; for example in St Gilles and in the church of St Mary. The latter has six burial places of Hanseatic merchants still to be seen, two tombs of which remain:[33] Rutger and Herman Runghe, perhaps father and son, who died after 1493. The epigraphs run:

> *Hier light Herman Runghe, Henderycx seune, Poorter te Lubeke van der Duytscher Huuse; sie starf up den iv dach van September . . .*
>   *Hier light begraven Rotgert Ruughe, Hendrycx seune, Poorter te Lubeke van den Duytsche huuse. Bidt voor de Zielen.*

Here lies Herman Runghe, son of Henderyc, citizen of Lübeck of the German Hanse who died September 4th.
Here lies Rotger Rughe, sone of Hendryc, citizen of Lübeck of the German Hanse. Pray for their souls.

The Hanseatic merchant and elderman of long standing, Jan Diercoop, was buried at St Gillis in 1495; he had been its churchwarden. In his will and testament he decreed a mass, another sacramental service, a meal for the poor serving 60 persons as well as the payment of certain amounts of money to the two large parish churches of the Holy Virgin and St Salvator.[34]

Apart from the large monasteries, there existed a number of smaller convents and other institutions that regularly received gifts. Here the fixed dates were also Midwinter and Good Friday. The *Leitfaden* mentions bedridden sick people and simple poor, the prisoners in the Steen, or jail, in addition to the sisters at Bethany at the end of Carmerstraat, the sisters' house *in den Castanienboom*, the women inhabiting the cathedral chapter in *Ganzestraat*, which was founded by some people from the order of the Grey Sisters in Oude Zak, and, finally, one anchoress at the Bogards.[35] In addition, the last wills and testaments of Hanseatic merchants reveal that a multitude of other institutions or private persons received gifts. Especially guilds and brotherhoods are recorded;[36] for instance, the Carmelites accommodated the brotherhood of Roosebeke, established on a pilgrim site of the same name.[37] It was founded in 1396 or shortly before; Hanseatic merchants participated in that as well. The Carmelites also accommodated the Scottish Brotherhood of St Ninian (founded in 1366), the brotherhood of the Immaculate Conception (1438), and that of The Holy Spirit. The brotherhood *van den Droghen Boome* (founded at the end of the 14th century) found a place with the Franciscans and at least six Easterlings were among its members. Furthermore, the last wills and decrees of Hanseatic merchants again and again contain references to different craftsmen guilds, especially the most important guilds of the textile trade, the *culcstickers* (tapestry embroiderers) and the *rijkepijnders* (port labourers).[38] They are frequently mentioned in connection with the donation of meals for the poor.

Within the Hanseatic agency, its office bearers were highly regarded for their generosity to religious and community organisations. Evidently there existed a connection between holding office in the agency, working actively in the religious field and being a member of a guild. This applies to eldermen and jurors, but particularly to the secretaries, who held a special position because of their specific duties and their unlimited terms of office.[39]

Other agencies of the Hanseatic League

The living conditions and private dealings of the merchants in Bruges have been no more extensively analysed than those in Bergen, London and Novgorod. Thus we can only point to the appropriate works of Stuart Jenks about London, Friedrich Bruns about Bergen, Jelena Rybina and Wolfgang Schlüter about Novgorod.

Peter's Guard in Novgorod, the foundation of which goes back to the 13th century, formed a self-contained area by the River Wolchow.[40] Its *Skra* (the statute), which has been passed on in seven versions, provides interesting insights into the inner court routine, legislation and the life of the merchants. The individual decrees again and again express the self-contained character of the merchant community and its separation from the local residents. One learns from the fourth and fifth versions of the *Skra* (14th century), that the agency had a church of its own, St Peter, which was closed to the Russians and had its own priest. Furthermore, those from Lübeck and Visby took turns in presenting the priest each year (*Vortmer de van Lubeke unde de van Gotlande scolen hir setten den prester malch sin jar*).[41] The church was not under any bishop or sovereign but was regarded as the property of the German merchants, a 'classic example of a traders' church, ... a free traders' church'.[42] At the same time, St Peter's served as a store.[43] The place where goods could be stored was determined in the *Skra*: the choir, for example, was reserved for wine, though the altar itself was excluded. Goods were not allowed to be moved during mass or traded inside the church. Similarly, the church's treasure, the religious objects (which included a precious painting) and the merchants' scales, were kept there. So it seems quite natural that the church also kept the St Peter-box, which, being the archive, contained the seals, documents and the *Skra* itself. Two merchants were locked up inside the church as night-watchmen and the eldermen received the key. The latter also selected the two eldermen of the church, who were responsible for the church coffers, the maintenance and security of the church. The income was generated through the *schot*, a turnover tax, which was higher in the more lucrative winter than in summer. Even the rents from the houses as well as one third of the court income, were paid to the church, and there were fees for the use of a wax-melting pot and a brewing vat. When the German merchants left Novgorod, they took these valuables and money with them. They were kept in the church of St Mary in Visby where there was also a St Peter's-box.

It is known from trade agreements between the Germans and the Russians that St Peter's in Novgorod had a graveyard of its own where merchants were buried. Priests working at the church came and went with the merchants and their duties included the writing of private and business letters for which they were paid extra. When the *steven*, or meeting of the merchants took place, it was announced in church.

In Bergen, the Hanseatic centre, the *Tyskebrygge*, was also a closed area. Around the middle of the 14th century the agency had been consolidated here. A close association between the Germans and a single church is evident. Their own parish church of St Mary's, which was situated close to the houses of the merchant community, was chosen by a number of *Bergenfahrer* as their burial place. Their last wills and testaments were analysed by Friedrich Bruns.[44] The church of St Mary's is constructed of stone and extensive parts of the wooden *Gaarden* have partly survived to this day. Within St Mary's church there was the chapel of the Bergenfahrer, including the altar of St Olaf. Lübeck had the privilege of appointing the priest and curates for the German merchants. The German guild worshipped St Catherine and St Dorothy. Two poor-houses were donated by the merchants. Among those churches that received testamentary gifts from the *Bergenfahrer*, who were mostly from Lübeck, were St Catherine's, All Saints', Holy Cross, St Michael's, the mendicant orders, some smaller convents and different guilds of the town. Frequently, some provision was made for the poor. On looking through some of the last wills and testaments, the rich social and religious life of these Hanseatic merchants emerges. Though there existed a close relationship with one single church, the personal contacts of individual merchants included a great many smaller or bigger churches, monasteries and guilds.

In London, the Steelyard - an area on the banks of the River Thames - was the centre of activity for the Germans. In the seventies of the 12th century, merchants from Cologne bought the Guildhall, a very large stone building. It would seem, however, that the Germans purchased other properties beyond this area and that their houses were spread across the Dowgate quarter.[45] Their religious life was concentrated on the parish church which was near, but just outside, the Steelyard. The church of All Hallows the Great (called the sailors' church in the 12th century) was used by both the locals of Dowgate and the Germans. Two thirds of the merchants identified from the testaments were buried there and almost all of them left a legacy to the church.[46] Every year, on St Barbara's Day (4th of December), a requiem was read for the deceased Hanseatic traders, followed by a banquet. The last wills and testaments published and analysed by Jenks show legacies to other churches and monasteries in London, but they were located in the close vicinity of the Steelyard. English people were chosen as executors as well and, in some cases, only English people. The executors, however, did not come from the immediate neighbourhood of the Steelyard, the rather poor Dowgate quarter, but were wealthy business contacts. The clergy of All Hallows, too, were called on as executors by the Hanseatic merchants.

Jenks has analysed Hanseatic wills and testaments for London but this has not been done for Bergen and Novgorod. A problem for this subject is that the available texts are public or official sources: the *Leitfaden*, the *Skra* and last wills and testaments. So, as there are no other written sources, only physical ones can be used to gain complementary information; one example is the memorial slab of the German, Wissel Smalenburg, which we are going to look at this afternoon.

Notes

[1] Albert Way, 'Engraved Sepulchral Slabs', *The Archaeological Journal*, 7, 1850, pp. 48-55, here p. 54; Herbert Haines, *A Manual of Monumental Brasses, Comprising an Introduction to the Study of these Memorials, and a List of Those Remaining in the British Isles.* 2 vol., London - Oxford 1861, Reprint Bath 1970, pp. xxiii f., n 1; Alan Coates Bouquet, *Church Brasses, British & Continental, with some Notes on Incised Stone Slabs and Indents.* London 1956, p. 7 with fig. p.8.

[2] Haines, *Manual* (like n 1), p. xxiv, n 1.

[3] Fig. after Malcolm W. Norris, *Brass Rubbing.* London 1965, pp. 48 ff.

[4] Otto Buchner, 'Zur Tiersymbolik, namentlich auf Grabmälern', *Zeitschrift für christliche Kunst* 16, 1903, pp. 369-380; Michel Pastoureau, 'Le Bestiaire des morts: présence animale sur les monuments funéraire (Xe - XIVe siècle)', in: *La figuration des morts dans la Chrétienté médiévale jusqu'à la fin du premier quart du XIVe siècle* (Cahiers de Fontevraud 1), Longué 1989, pp. 124-137.

[5] Memoria in the Hanseatic area: Stuart Jenks, *Hansische Vermächtnisse in London: ca. 1363-1483*, HGbll, 104, 1986, pp. 35-111; Dietrich Poeck, 'Totengedenken in Hansestädten', in: *Vinculum societatis, dedicated to Joachim Wollasch*, ed. Franz Neiske, Dietrich Poeck and Mechthild Sandmann, Sigmaringendorf 1991, pp. 175-232; Dietrich W. Poeck, 'Rat und Memoria', in: *Memoria in der Gesellschaft des Mittelalters*, ed. Dieter Geuenich and Otto Gerhard Oexle (Veröffentlichungen des Max-Planck-Instituts für Geschichte 111), Göttingen 1994, pp. 286-335.

[6] Walter Stein, *Die Genossenschaft der deutschen Kaufleute zu Brügge in Flandern.* Berlin 1890; Volker Henn, 'Das Brügger Kontor', in: *Die Hanse. Lebenswirklichkeit und Mythos.* Catalogue Museum für Hamburgische Geschichte, 1, Hamburg 1989, pp.160-164. - Memoria in Bruges: Herman J. Leloux, 'De Oosterlingen en andere vreemde kooplieden te Brugge en kerkelijke en sociaal-caritatieve instellingen', *Annales de la Société d'Emulation de Bruges* CX, 1973, pp. 21-39; Renée Rößner, *Tod, Begräbnis, Gedächtnis der Hansekaufleute in Brügge.* M.A. thesis (ms.), Kiel 1992.

[7] Anke Greve, *Gastgeber der Hanse: Die Brügger Wirte im 14. Jahrhundert.* Staatsexamenarbeit (ms.), Kiel 1990; - shortly: Anke Greve, 'Herberge, Wirte und Handel im Spätmittelalter', in:

Rolf Hammel-Kiesow/Werner Paravicini (edd.), *Stand und Aufgaben der hansischen Geschichtsforschung.* Cologne 1999.

[8] Rößner, Tod (like n 6), pp. 31 f., with further literature.

[9] Rößner, Tod (like n 6), p. 34.

[10] HUB III, Nr. 497 § 28 and HUB II, Nr. 154 § 20; - Cf. Rößner, Tod (like n 6), p. 35 and last: Peter Stützel, *Die Privilegien des deutschen Kaufmanns in Brügge im 13 und 14,* Jahrhundert, HGbll. 116, 1998, pp. 23-63, esp. pp. 47 f.

[11] Cf. for the following: Rößner, Tod (like n 6), pp. 35-37.

[12] HUB VIII ed. Walther Stein, Leipzig 1899, Nr. 823, pp. 515 f.; Nr. 526 § 1, p. 344; cf. here, n 30.

[13] HUB VIII, Nr. 434, p. 285 ff.

[14] HR I, ed. Karl Koppmann, 2, Leipzig 1872, Nr. 98 § 1-2, pp. 111 f.

[15] HUB XI, ed. Walther Stein, 1916, Nr. 1234, pp. 759-774; - the author of the text was identified as mag. Gerard Bruens from Deventer; cf. Herman Leloux, *Kirche und Caritas im Leben der Genossenschaft des deutschen Kaufmanns zu Brügge,* HGbll. 91, 1973, pp. 34-45, esp. p. 39, n 19; Herman Leloux, Zum mittelniederländischen 'Leitfaden für die Älterleute des deutschen Kaufmanns zu Brügge' aus dem Jahre 1500, *Studia Germanica Gandensia 14,* 1973, pp. 145-159.

[16] J.H. Beuken, *De Hanze en Vlaanderen.* Maastricht 1950, pp. 37 f.; Jos. Marechal, 'De betrekkingen tussen Karmelieten en Hanzeaten te Brugge van 1347 tot 1523', in: Jos. Marechal, *Europese aanwezigheid te Brugge. De vreemde kolonies (XIVde - XIXde eeuw),* Bruges 1985, pp. 63-81. First in: *Handelingen van het Genootschap voor Geschiedenis 100,* 1963 (1965), pp. 206-227; Rößner, Tod (like n 6), pp. 52 ff.; Heinz Stoob, *Die Hanse.* Graz - Vienna - Cologne 1995, p. 147; Stützel, Privilegien (like n 10), p. 47.

[17] HR II, ed. Goswin FRHR. von der Ropp, 7, Leipzig 1892, Nr. 261, pp. 442 f. (1475 Jan. 3); cf. Nr. 247, p. 428.

[18] HR II, 3, Leipzig 1881, Nr. 345 § 5, p. 251.

[19] Karl Koppmann (ed.), *Leitfaden für die Aelterleute des Deutschen Kaufmanns zu Brügge,* Hamburg 1875, p. 25.

[20] *Leitfaden,* chapter 11.

[21] Cf. Leloux, *Kirche und Caritas* (like n 15), p. 37, n 10.

[22] *Leitfaden,* chapter 13.

[23] *Leitfaden,* chapter 15.

[24] *Leitfaden,* chapter 18-19.

[25] *Leitfaden,* chapter 20-21.

[26] HUB X, ed. Walther Stein, Leipzig 1907, Nr. 1217, pp. 733 f.

[27] HUB IX, Nr. 689, § 4-5.

[28] HUB X, Nr. 905, p. 563 f. (OFM), Nr. 960, p. 593 f. (OP), HUB XI, Nr. 16, p. 13 f. (OESA); cf. Leitfaden, chapter 46.

[29] HUB IV, Nr. 509, pp. 210 f.; cf. Rößner, Tod (like n 6), pp. 59 f.

[30] HUB VIII, Nr. 823, p. 515 f.; cf. Rößner, Tod (like n 6), pp. 36, 60. - Names of the Hanseatics: Tydemann Blomenrod († before 1359), Tydemann von Danzig († after 1367), Heynric Symon († 1393), Arnoud van Hasselen († after 1415), Jan van dem Borne († before 1459). None of these is mentioned at Valentin Vermeersch, *Grafmonumenten te Brugge voor 1578.* 3 vol., Bruges 1976.

[31] Rößner, Tod (like n 6), pp. 61 ff.

[32] Leloux, *Kirche und Caritas* (like n 15), p. 39.

[33] Rößner, Tod (like n 6), pp. 62 f., 133 f.; Jean Jacques Gailliard, *Inscriptions funéraires et monumentales de la Flandre Occidentale avec des donnés historiques et généalogiques.* 3 vol.; Bruges 1861-1887, II, p. 164; Vermeersch, *Grafmonumenten* (like n 30), III, Nr. 360, pp. 401-403.

[34] HUB XI, Nr. 807, pp. 520 ff.; cf. Rößner, Tod (like n 6), p. 63.

³⁵ *Leitfaden*, chapter 31; cf. Rößner, Tod (like n 6), pp. 64 ff.

³⁶ Rößner, Tod (like n 6), pp. 66 ff.

³⁷ William Henry James Weale, 'La procession et les confréries de Notre Dame de Roosebeke', *La Flandre 3*, 1869-1870, pp. 154-187.

³⁸ *Rijkepijnders*: cf. Stützel, *Privilegien* (like n 10), p. 46.

³⁹ Rößner, Tod (like n 6), p. 70.

⁴⁰ Philippe Dollinger, *Die Hanse*, Stuttgart ⁴1989, pp. 133 ff., Norbert Angermann, 'Nowgorod', in: *Die Hanse. Lebenswirklichkeit und Mythos*. Catalogue Museum für Hamburgische Geschichte, 1, Hamburg 1989, pp. 172-176.

⁴¹ Wolfgang Schlüter (ed.), Die *Nowgoroder Schra in sieben Fassungen vom 13. bis zum 17.* Jahrhundert. Dorpat 1914, IV.68; cf. V.79 (p. 144). Cf. ibid. IV.21 *(Weret oc sake, dat de copman utvore, so moghen VI mesterman unde IX knechte ... de kerken open holden ...)*, V.29 (p. 134), IV.10 *(Vortmer weret, dat jeman unlust dede under der missen, et were wormede et were, de breke 1 marc.)*,V.18 (p. 132). VI.1 (pp. 177 f.) enumerates the objects that were stolen by the Russians in 1494, especially the liturgical equipment that had been owned by the German merchants.

⁴² Paul Johansen, *Die Kaufmannskirche im Ostseegebiet, in: Studien zu den Anfängen des europäischen Städtewesens (Vorträge und Forschungen 4)*, Sigmaringen ⁴1975, pp. 499-525, esp. p. 499; - cf. Karlheinz Blaschke, *Nikolaipatrozinium und städtische Frühgeschichte*, ZRG KA 53, 1967, pp. 273-337, esp. p. 313.

⁴³ For the following: Johansen, *Kaufmannskirche* (like n 42), p. 500 ff.

⁴⁴ Friedrich BRUNS, *Die Lübecker Bergenfahrer und ihre Chronistik* (Hansische Geschichtsquellen, N.F. 2), Berlin 1900, pp. CXXV ff.; - to the agency: Dollinger, *Hanse* (like n 40), pp. 136 f. and Carsten Müller-Boysen, 'Das Bergener Kontor und die hansischen Niederlassungen in Tönsberg und Oslo', in: *Die Hanse. Lebenswirklichkeit und Mythos*. Catalogue Museum für Hamburgische Geschichte, 1, Hamburg 1989, pp. 165-171.

⁴⁵ J.M. Lappenberg, *Urkundliche Geschichte des hansischen Stahlhofes zu London*. Hamburg 1851, p. 72; Jochen Goetze, 'Statuten des Stahlhofs in London, 1388-1460', in: *Quellen zur Hanse-Geschichte*, ed. Rolf Sprandel (FSGA 36), Darmstadt 1982, pp. 350-382; Dollinger, *Hanse* (like n 40), pp. 137 ff.; Derek Keene, 'Ein Haus in London: Von der Guildhall zum Stalhof', in: *Die Hanse. Lebenswirklichkeit und Mythos*. Catalogue Museum für Hamburgische Geschichte, 1, Hamburg 1989, pp. 46-49; Derek Keene, *Die deutsche Guildhall und ihre Umgebung*. Ibid., pp. 149-156; Stuart Jenks, *Leben im Stalhof*. Ibid., pp. 157-159; Rößner, Tod (like n 6), pp. 81 f.

⁴⁶ Jenks, *Hansische Vermächtnisse* (like n 5); Jenks, *Leben im Stalhof* (like n 45), p. 158.

LYNN AND THE HANSE

Trade and Relations in the Middle Ages*

by

Stuart Jenks

Once the preliminary skirmishes were over, the English diplomats charged by Edward IV with negotiating an end to the war with the Hanse put a serious offer on the table on the 19th and 20th of July 1473.[1] They offered blanket compensation for all Hanseatic losses and injuries, which was to be reckoned against the customs due on Hanseatic merchandise,[2] and asked their counterparts to name a figure. After some deliberations, the Hanseatic delegation stated that, while the losses on their side in fact amounted to £200,000, they would be content to accept £25,000, provided Edward IV granted them title to the Steelyards in London and Boston and to a house in Lynn.[3] After a certain amount of haggling, the Hanseatic demand was granted and duly embodied in the Peace of Utrecht on the 28th of February 1474.[4] The title to the Lynn property was transferred to the Hanse on the 29th of April 1475.[5]

Now, it is extremely odd that Lynn should feature so prominently in the first specific conditions the Hanse named for peace with England. In the first place, in contrast to London and Boston, there was no Steelyard in Lynn, that is to say no property owned or rented by an organized body of Hanseatic merchants in common. Moreover, the English position in Utrecht was extremely weak. Edward's chances of reconquering Normandy and Gascony in alliance with Burgundy – the cornerstone of English foreign policy since 1466[6] – were nil, unless he could achieve a settlement with the Hanse.[7] Indeed, the king's instructions to his diplomats made it very clear that they were, in the end, to concede anything the Hanse wanted rather than jeopardize the peace.[8] Now, if the Hanseatic diplomats had the English over a barrel in Utrecht, why did they, from the very beginning, ask for a house in Lynn when they could have had one in virtually any English town? Why did Lynn feature so prominently in the Hanse's conditions for peace?

In order to solve this problem, we are going to have to take a long trawl through Anglo-Hanseatic history and address two basic questions: First, what was the Hanse? And, second, what role did Lynn play in Hanseatic commerce and diplomacy up to the Peace of Utrecht in 1474?

1. What was the Hanse?

What, then, was the Hanse? The question is deceptively simple. In order to answer it, we have to begin by placing the Hanse in the context of the political realities of the late medieval Empire. The salient fact is the concentration of royal government in the South of Germany from around 1250. The imperial government really didn't have much choice in the matter. The territorial possessions of the Saxon dynasty (919-1024) had long since been squandered away by their South German successors. Consequently, the crown had virtually no power base in the North from which to control and direct developments. To be sure, it might hope to consolidate and expand its position in the North by seizing opportunities as they came along – Barbarossa and Frederick II being adept practitioners of the art[9] – but by the mid-13th century the imperial government just gave up: its resources were so limited and its chances of success so slim that it just wasn't worth trying. This, in turn, bred bland indifference. Consequently, those living in the North could expect no support at all from the imperial government. If they got into difficulties, they were on their own. Now, this had important consequences for the emerging Hanse.[10] Royal inaction forced the towns to take over many activities which contemporaries thought of as royal prerogatives.[11] But the towns had to face stiff competition from the territorial princes for possession of the prerogatives which the emperors let slip from their grasp. In Northern Germany this led to a long, desperate and, at least in the Middle Ages, inconclusive struggle between the cities and the princes. The towns had to be continually on their guard against the attempts of their titular lords to reduce their autonomy and their economic freedom of movement. It was natural that towns threatened by grasping and ambitious lords should pool their resources. Thus, the Hanse was in essence the result of a series of stopgap measures designed to repulse the territorial princes and to ward off the economic calamities which regularly resulted from the continuous feuds of the magnates.[12]

However, resistance to the princes was only one half of the consensus upon which the Hanse was founded. Just as important was the towns' desire to put an end to the depredations of pirates and robbers in the northern European commercial arteries and to secure adequate legal protection for their merchants in the markets to which they travelled.[13] In the face of the indifference of the imperial government, the towns were forced to negotiate on their own with foreign and domestic princes for legal, fiscal and commercial privileges. Once they succeeded, of course, the towns had to redouble their efforts to ensure that their rights were not emasculated or abrogated.

Of course, the Hanseatic desire for optimum conditions for commerce coupled with the complete autonomy of the individual towns at the cost of a minimum of force was merely the lowest common denominator.[14] The devil, as always, lurked in the details. Every town had to decide at a given point whether the short-term losses it would surely suffer, if it were, for instance, to join in boycotting England, would be balanced out by the long-term gains, if the English were to knuckle under and grant new and improved privileges, which would bolster the economic position of all Hanseatic merchants. Thus, at any point, one can always find towns that pursued policies directly contrary to the resolutions of the Hanseatic Diet. The conflict between self-interest and the common cause, between short-term profits and long-term gains, was woven into the fabric of the Hanse from the very beginning. Thus, the closer one looks at the Hanse, the more chimerical it reveals itself to be. It could only fill the stage left vacant by the emperors and take an active role in international politics (which was vitally important for trade) if enough member cities were in basic agreement on what to do about a certain matter. If no agreement could be reached, then nothing happened. Consequently, what we think of as the 'Hanse' is actually a continuously shifting coalition of towns with roughly compatible overall goals, but, at any given moment, widely differing interests and tactics.[15] In fact, the Hanse was a bit like a kaleidoscope: the slightest twist in international affairs instantly produced a completely new constellation of towns.

This is not to say that chaos reigned. All Hanseatic towns had long-term interests and trading partners, with whom relations ranged from intimate co-operation to bitter, even violent rivalry. Generally speaking, Hanseatic politics turned on the question of whose economic interests were affected by a given development. Of course, towns whose trade was not threatened could afford to view matters with considerable detachment. But whatever happened in England or indeed in Lynn itself, there were sure to be chortling winners and losers screaming bloody murder. This, in turn, means that in a very real sense there were no relations at all between Lynn and 'the Hanse'. Lynn had very close relations with some Hanseatic towns, and none at all with the vast majority.[16] The crucial questions for us are: Just who were Lynn's Hanseatic trading partners? And how did Lynn's relationship with these towns develop over the course of the Middle Ages?

2. Lynn and the Hanse to 1474

Lynn's relations with the towns of the Hanse can be neatly divided into two periods, one before, and the other after the mid-14th century. These two periods could not be more dissimilar: between 1350 and 1380 the structure of Lynn's Hanseatic trade changed completely, as one group of Hanseatic visitors from Lübeck was supplanted by another from Prussia.

Our first firm evidence for the presence of German merchants in England comes from the late 12th century. For some time, the Flemish had been exporting their cloth to Germany,[17] but were unable to find return freight of interest to the English, from whom they bought the wool essential to their cloth industry. From 1165 onwards, Flemish merchants made repeated attempts to regain access to the wine country of the Upper Rhine, which had been closed to them when Cologne began to erect a staple in the mid-12th century. Clearly, the Flemish wanted to establish a profitable trade circuit, whereby they would export cloth to Germany, buy wine and ship it to England, where they could purchase English wool and bring it to Flanders.[18] However, Cologne managed to defend its staple by appealing to Henry II, who was more than happy to have Cologne as a counterweight to Flanders. In 1175/76, Cologne merchants obtained a safe conduct,[19] protection for their guildhall in London[20] and, most importantly, the right to sell their wine in London in the same market and for the same price as the wines the Flemish imported from France.[21] Although the Flemish continued to export cloth to the English fairs and buy wool, their expansion into German markets had been checked, and Cologne had gained a firm foothold in the lucrative London market.[22]

After the turn of the century, other German merchants began to frequent English markets. At times only vaguely described as merchants of the Emperor and the Duke of Saxony,[23] at others clearly identifiable as men of Lübeck, Hamburg, Bremen and Staveren,[24] these merchants avoided London and landed in Boston, Lynn and Southampton.[25] While our evidence is sparse (and we have little more than royal orders to release German ships which had been arrested as Flemish), it is suggestive. Boston, Lynn and Southampton all offered easy access by river to the major English fairs.[26] The fact that the men of the Emperor had been arrested as Flemings, who had long frequented English fairs,[27] in ports offering easy access to those very fairs, suggests that the Easterlings, who were firmly established in Bruges by the mid 13th century,[28] had followed the Flemish to England and begun to visit the fairs themselves, exporting the English goods they bought at those fairs to Flanders. Indeed, there is a certain amount of evidence that this was the case. In 1267, merchants from Lynn, Canterbury, Gascony and Germany chartered a ship in common, in order to export wool, wine, lead and other goods they had bought at the Bury St Edmunds fair via Lynn to Flanders.[29] During the Boston fair in 1271, sixteen Lübeck wool exporters gathered under the wing of the Alderman of the Roman Empire in Lynn, who sealed a recognizance for £200 to cover the 'new aid' on the wool they had bought at the fair.[30] In 1287 Lübeck merchants were exporting Flemish cloth and spices to Lynn,[31] and in 1303 Boston fair suggested itself as the obvious place for Westphalian merchants from London and sea captains from Rostock and Lübeck to meet.[32]

While the Easterlings did not entirely supplant the Flemish as suppliers of English goods to the continent, Hanseatic trade in and through Lynn was nonetheless considerable. If, as seems reasonable to assume, Prince Edward's 'new aid' represented a 15th,[33] then the wool the Lübeck merchants bought at Boston fair in 1271 was worth some £3000; in 1291 a representative of Edward I alleged that 140 ships had failed to pay lastage in Lynn in the last eight years,[34] and in 1302, 22 Hanseatic cogs arrived in Lynn with stockfish.[35]

However important they might have been, the Easterlings were not the only merchants to frequent Lynn in the 13th century. The Norwegians conducted a substantial trade, importing stockfish and cod-liver oil and exporting wool to Flanders.[36]The men of Gotland imported Swedish metals,[37] furs from Novgorod and other Eastern merchandise to the fairs: even at the beginning of the 14th century, when Visby's trade had been largely eclipsed and the fairs had entered their final, if gentle decline, the royal wardrobe still bought most of its furs from Gotland merchants at the fairs of Boston and Ely.[38]

As the 13th century drew to a close, however, momentous changes were afoot in Lynn's trade. Not only were the fairs, hitherto a major factor in Lynn's prosperity, in decline,[39] but the Flemish had also ceased to play a leading role in English commerce and the merchants from Gotland and Norway had been largely, if not completely, supplanted. What evidence we have suggests that it was Lübeck and its neighbouring towns who inherited their position in Lynn's foreign trade. Finally, Lynn's own merchants had begun their determined expansion eastwards, their first goal being to break into the trade in stockfish and cod-liver oil in the Norwegian staple town of Bergen.[40] The upshot was the first serious conflict between Lynn and the Hanse. At the end of the trading season in 1302, the London Steelyard decreed a boycott of Lynn. The Hanseatic complaints[41]were the usual ones: Lynn had forbidden alien merchants from trading with one another and had limited them to wholesale trading in stockfish, wax, furs, potash, sturgeon and herring. Warehousing of grain prior to export had been forbidden, Lynn merchants had failed to make good on contracts and had been loath to pay for goods purchased on credit. Finally, the Steelyard complained about Lynn's management of the royal prise of stockfish in 1302 and its imposition of double murage on aliens. The dispute was finally settled to the Hanse's satisfaction in 1310,[42]after a second boycott which has left its traces only in the customs material.

Thereafter, conflicts were rare and not very serious. Indeed, most of our information on Lynn's relations with the Hanse comes from the customs accounts. Owen's edition of the accounts for 1322/23[43] gives us an opportunity to analyse Lynn's foreign trade during this period (Table 1). Well over half the alien imports consisted of stockfish from Bergen, salted herring from Scania and iron and steel from Sweden. These were the typical bulky wares of classic Hanseatic east-west trade; by contrast, trade with Flanders was far less important. The aliens' exports tell the same tale: well over half consisted of cloth, distantly followed by wool, ale and lead. Finally, those foreign merchants we can identify came overwhelmingly from Lübeck and Visby. While the customs accounts are silent on indigenous commerce,[44] scattered evidence does tend to confirm our impression that Lynn's traders were also oriented towards the east, principally Bergen.

Lynn, Alien Imports and Exports, 20 July 1322-1 October 1323[45]

Imports	Value (in £)	Exports	Value (in £)
herring	832.5	cloth	1101
stockfish	785.166	ale	224
steel	646	lead	215
hemp	210	worsteds, sayes	186.5
alum	205	cash	172.5
woad	203	coal, sea coal	32.75
lumber (pine, righolt, tunholt)	188.5	salt	21
mills, handmills, millstones	136.333	honey	16
fur	123.5	seeds	16
iron	112	rope	7
estrich boards	106.333	wine	6
potash	82.75	catskins	3
grain (barley, wheat, rye, oats)	80	herring	2.5
pitch, rosin	63.833	slipstones	2.5
salt	50	cheese	1.25
leather	32.916	mills	.5
masts	27.6		
spars	24		
Frisian cloth	21		
cotton	20		
skins	19.16		

onions & garlic	18	
sturgeon	15.5	
fruit	12.25	
bacon	10	
fish	9	
flax	9	
cash	7.5	
staves	6.5	
haddock	4.5	
troughs	3	
whetstones	3	
oil	2	
nuts	1.75	
clipping	1	
eels	.75	
swans	.66	
cloth	[5 pieces][46]	
wax	[67 quintals][47]	
Total	**£4073.759**	**£2036.5**

By mid century, however, the first period of Lynn's relations with the Hanse was drawing to a close. In November 1353 Lynn ceased to be a wool staple port.[48] Wool traders and Lübeck merchants alike decamped to Boston, taking the wool and stockfish trade with them. Indeed, since the royal customs administration lumped Lynn together with Boston, there is no customs material at all to work from: we have virtually no information on Lynn's trade until 1373, when Lynn re-emerged as a separate customs district.[49] But by then, everything had changed. No longer was alien trade dominated by Lübeck and Visby: rather, Prussian merchants, chiefly from Danzig, were now the most numerous and prominent Hanseatic visitors. Lynn's own merchants had not abandoned Bergen, but it was no longer a market of the first rank. Rather, Lynn's commerce was pressing inexorably eastwards. By 1375 merchants from Lynn were complaining about their treatment at the Scania fairs,[50] and by 1385 they had established a commercial beachhead in Prussia.[51]

Here, the English were spectacularly successful. From the 1380s onwards, they controlled 80-90% of Anglo-Prussian trade.[52] By 1425 they had a lockhold not only on the export of English cloth but also on retail cloth sales in Danzig itself, which resident Englishmen dominated. And Lynn merchants played a leading role in this success story. In all the lists of English losses in trade with Prussia – and they cover the years 1370 to 1388, c. 1388 to 1436 and 1474 to 1491[53]– Lynn merchants led the pack, usually with about a third of all English damages and with a rising tendency. It is not surprising then, to learn that the men of Lynn played a prominent role in the English colony in Danzig. Indeed, a tour of duty in Danzig would seem to have been a normal part of the commercial education of a Lynn merchant, if the number of apprentices absent in Prussia when their masters requested the freedom of the city for them is any indication.[54] So heavily were Lynn merchants involved in trade with Prussia that they were regarded as experts. Every single English embassy which negotiated with the Hanse in the 15th century included a Lynn merchant. Indeed, in 1408, Henry IV ordered Lynn to send a delegation post haste to the council in London, since Prussian delegates had arrived and, as the king said, 'The men of Lynn understand commerce in Prussia better than any other merchants of the realm.'[55]

Of course, success bred resentment. The total volume of Anglo-Prussian trade was immense, but Prussian merchants didn't even have a look-in. From their perspective, English merchants were simply invincible: in 1396 the Prussian towns complained that the English were ruining the country with their merchandise,[56] and in 1438 Danzig warned that the English had so much money and merchandise that they would completely dominate trade and even make Prussia a colony like Gascony.[57] Throughout the 15th century, Danzig merchants despaired of garnering a significant portion of trade with England as long as their English rivals had a foot in the door in Prussia.[58] But the English were not happy either. From the late 14th century onwards, English merchants and diplomats alike had demanded rights in Prussia comparable to those enjoyed by Hanseatic merchants in England.[59] Unsurprisingly then, Prussia was the flashpoint of all Anglo-Hanseatic disputes. All of the conflicts with Danzig about trade were complicated by the fact that Danzig's lord, the High Master of the Teutonic Order, was much given to granting English demands in order to discipline Danzig, the largest and most independent-minded Prussian town. Of course, whenever the Order was weak, Danzig put the screws on the English.[60] Sharp practice, disputes about debts, freight charges and shipwreck all fuelled resentment. While it would be wrong to believe that Lynn was without friends in Danzig and Danzig had none in Lynn, the hotheads had definitely gotten the upper hand. Whereas Lynn had heavily favoured a settlement with Prussia in 1409,[61] it agitated for curtailment of Hanseatic privileges in 1423. In 1436, Lynn and Hull - the towns most prominent in trade with Prussia and chiefly responsible for the depredations wreaked on Prussian merchants - spread poisonous rumours in order to scuttle a treaty with the Hanse,[62] but were the first to take advantage of the opportunities in Prussia after the Treaty of London was signed on 22 March 1437.[63]

In theory, this treaty resolved a number of issues to the satisfaction of both parties. It not only removed all restrictions on commerce, including the prohibition of trading with non-natives[64] - a sore point with the English -

but also silenced Hanseatic protests that the imposition of poundage in England ran contrary to its privileges by permitting only such duties as had been continuously collected for at least a century.[65] Now, while the diplomats regarded the rights anchored in the treaty as nothing more than customary,[66] English merchants in Prussia demanded that they be granted any and all rights which – in the light of English demands for reciprocity – could possibly be interpreted into the treaty.[67] In particular, they protested that the collection of poundage and harbour duties in Prussia – neither more than a century old – was now prohibited by treaty.[68] Needless to say, the Prussian authorities rejected these English demands out of hand. Moreover, they refused to ratify the treaty, since subsequent developments had only confirmed the dolorous experience of all Prussians: whatever happened, it only redounded to the advantage of the English.[69]

Despite all the pressure the English brought to bear, Danzig remained firm: the English were welcome to come to Danzig on an equal footing with all other non-Prussian Hanseatic merchants, but the Treaty of London had granted them no new rights.[70] In particular, there was to be no corporate organization of the English merchants with internal jurisdiction, no freedom from customs and harbour duties, no retail trade and no direct dealing with non-Prussians.

Nonetheless, Lynn's Prussian trade throve. Turnover averaged just under £5000 a year until the capture of the Bay fleet in 1449.[71] The ensuing imprisonment of all English merchants in Prussia[72] instantly halved the volume of trade. Then, in 1454, Danzig seceded from Prussia and placed itself under Polish suzerainty, receiving a charter from Kasimir II in 1457 giving it exclusive control over shipping and commerce.[73] While this did not affect the volume of trade with Lynn, it did shift its terms. Although Danzig was more than willing to grant Lynn shippers and merchants safe conducts for trade,[74] it was now free to deny any Englishmen the right of abode, and this destroyed the English cloth distribution system, which depended on resident factors. As a result, Prussian merchants for the first time in the 15th century consistently handled over half the traffic with Lynn.[75]

But the hardest blow to Lynn's Prussian trade came from another quarter altogether. Despite English and Danish prohibitions,[76] merchants from Lynn and other English towns had continued to trade directly with Iceland, in order to avoid the heavy charges due on Icelandic wares at the Bergen staple. This raised the spectre of Danish measures against English shipping passing through the Sound on its way to Prussia, about which Lynn had been concerned in 1429.[77] While nothing of the sort happened for quite some time, an incident in 1467 had massive repercussions. Merchants from Lynn and Bristol had murdered the Danish governor of Iceland and committed a number of other enormities.[78] In retaliation, the King of

Denmark seized six English ships bound for Prussia – two of them from Lynn[79] – while they were passing through the Sound in 1468.[80] Although King Christian made it clear that this measure was directed solely against Lynn and that other Englishmen were free and welcome to sail through the Sound,[81] the Nevills – as owners of one of the ships seized in the Sound[82] scarcely disinterested parties – were instrumental in having all Hanseatic merchants in England arrested by order of king and council.[83]

Subsequently, on the flimsy pretext that some Danzig sailors and shippers had taken part in the capture of the English ships, suit was filed before king and council against the entire Hanse for £20,000 in compensation.[84] Lübeck engaged the services of the best Roman lawyer available to refute the assertion that the Hanse as a whole was responsible for the depredations of certain individuals from Danzig,[85] but it did no good. In November 1468, the council condemned the Hanse to pay £20,000 in compensation.[86] For its part, the Hanse suspended trade with England,[87] recalled all Hanseatic merchants[88] and began preparations to fight England at sea.[89]

After both sides had exhausted themselves in the war[90] and the peace negotiations had begun, the Hanseatic delegates made it very plain that they regarded London, Lynn and Boston as the principal cause of all the strife which had sundered England and the Hanse since 1468.[91] Hence, they said, it was only right that these towns should cede the properties in question as compensation for all the ignominious injuries, harms and rebukes the Hanse had suffered at their hands.[92] No other measure proposed by the English, the Hanse's delegates said, was better suited to assuage Hanseatic feelings and create a true and lasting peace.[93]

That, then, is the explanation. The house across from St Margaret's Church was to be ceded to the Hanse as an expiatory offer, intended to effect a lasting reconciliation between Lynn and its Hanseatic trading partners.[94] And the Diet knew exactly who those partners were. In April of 1474, Danzig was asked to send a representative to take possession of the Lynn steelyard. The explanation was very simple: 'Your merchants', the Diet wrote, 'frequent Lynn more than any other Hanseatic merchants, and therefore this matter is of more concern to you than anyone else.'[95] It is fitting to note that, in the end, it was not Danzig merchants who took actual possession of the Steelyard, but their long-time friends in Lynn, Henry Baxter, Harry Patenmaker and Thomas Wright,[96] who had stuck to them loyally since the dark days of 1468.[97]

However, I must point out that the Hanse did not get precisely what it wanted in Lynn.[98] In July of 1473 the Hanse's delegates had demanded a house in Lynn, but had not specified any particular property,[99] other than to say that it should abut onto the Ouse.[100] It was only when the preliminary

Lynn waterfront in about 1730 with the Parish church of St Margaret as it would have appeared in the 15th century.

treaty was signed on the 13th of September 1473 that specifics were named. In Lynn, the Hanse was to receive 'a similar house in a certain street commonly called the Checker next the water'.[101] Now, the reasons for this are pretty plain. With a house abutting directly onto the Ouse, lighters could unload directly through the watergates and into the warehouses which were a common feature at the back of the houses which Lynn merchants had been building along the river bank from the 14th century onwards.[102] Moreover, a house in the Checker, today's King Street, would bring the Hanseatic merchants into close contact with the Lynn merchant community, which had become concentrated in the streets leading into Tuesday Market: King Street, St Nicholas Street and St Ann's Street.[103] The Hanse wanted to be where the action was.

However, getting there was not as easy as the Hanse thought. The English delegation stalled at first, claiming that it was not empowered to discuss such matters,[104] but its second objection was much more weighty.[105] Since the London Steelyard belonged to the City and the Lynn and Boston properties to private citizens, Edward couldn't simply grant them away,[106] but would have to 'call and have communicacion with the persones to whom they belanged'.[107] Since that was impossible in the short term, the matter would have to be adjourned until the next round of negotiations. And indeed, when Edward instructed his diplomats on the 20th December 1473, he insisted on one alteration to the preliminary treaty: the word 'Checker' would have to be struck from the text.[108] The reason was that the king was simply unable to find a house in the Checker to buy, as the Hanseatic delegation learned on the 7th of February 1474.[109] Consequently, the Peace of Utrecht stuck to the vague formulation of the preliminary treaty of the previous autumn: the Hanse would receive a house in Lynn next the water, but one which had yet to be specified, let alone bought.[110]

Walter Coney's house in the Saturday Market Place, built in about 1450.

However, there is another side to the matter. On the 3rd of November 1473 a privy seal letter from Edward IV regarding the mercantile treaty with the Easterlings was read before the Lynn congregation, which empowered a commission to negotiate with King and council.[111] Now, the makeup of the Lynn commission is extremely interesting. William Wales, the mayor, Walter Coney, an alderman, Thomas Leighton and Thomas Thoresby had all been involved in trade with Prussia for many years.[112] Indeed, Wales and Leighton had suffered losses when the Lynn ships had been seized in the Sound in 1468,[113] and Wales was named by several Danzig merchants as having received the goods seized from them in Lynn shortly thereafter.[114] While this might lead one to infer a certain measure of hostility to the Hanse, other facts point in the opposite direction. Thoresby and Coney were very closely connected to St Margaret's parish, both having provided funds for the repair of the church in 1472.[115] Indeed, Thoresby's house lay just to the north of the future Hanseatic Steelyard[116] while Cony had built a house on Saturday Market Place around 1450.[117] Moreover, Thoresby and Ceony knew all about the property, having witnessed the penultimate conveyance in 1468.[118] This suggests that, far from being hostile to the Hanse, Thoresby and Coney had a definite interest in enticing the Hanse away from the Checker and onto Saturday Market Place. On balance, then, it would seem that Lynn wanted the Hanse, and in particular its old trading partners from Danzig to re-establish a presence in Lynn. And it seems to me that this is confirmed by ensuing developments. Of all the East Coast towns which had had Hanseatic connections before the conflict, only Lynn re-established its Prussian trade after the Peace of Utrecht. To be sure, ships from Danzig continued to call at London and Hull, but active English participation in trade with Danzig up to the turn of the century was limited to merchants and shippers from Lynn.[119] The fact that Danzig accepted them shows, I think, that whatever lingering resentments might have been present on either side faded away before the enticing commercial prospects.

Notes

* This paper is reproduced in the same form as it was delivered. Only footnotes have been added. Abbreviations: HR 1 = Karl Koppmann (ed.), *Die Recesse und andere Akten der Hansetage von 1256-1430,* 8 vols, Leipzig 1870-1897; HR II = Goswin Freiherr von der Ropp (ed), *Hanserecesse von 1431-1476,* 7 vols, Leipzig 1876-1892; HR III = Dietrich Schäfer and Friedrich Techen (eds.), *Hanserecesse von 1477-1530,* 9 vols, 7 vols, Leipzig 1881-1913; HUB = Konstantin Höhlbaum et al. (eds.), *Hansisches Urkundenbuch,* 11 vols, Halle a.S. 1876; HR IV = Klaus Friedland and Gottfried Wentz (eds), *Hanserezesse von 1531 bis 1560,* 2 vols, Cologne - Vienna 1970.

[1] HUB 10.241 § 32-9 p. 147-9; cf. the Hanseatic report on the negotiations: HR II.7.34 § 36-42, p. 30-2.

[2] HUB 10.241 § 39, p. 149.

[3] HUB 10.241 § 40, p. 149; HR II.7.34 § 42, p. 32-3.

[4] HR II.7.142 § 8, p. 344-5. Cf. the agreement on the application of the Peace of Utrecht: HR II.7.143 § 3, p. 351-2 (28.Feb. 1474).

[5] HUB 10.411, p. 255. The original deed is transmitted in the Lübeck archives (AHL. Anglicana 209) and was copied onto the Patent Rolls (PRO, C66/535 m 6).

[6] Charles Ross, Edward IV, London 1974, p. 107ff, 205ff.

[7] Ross, Edward IV, p. 211.

[8] HR II.7.107 § 31, p. 219 (20. Dec. 1473): 'In all whiche poyntis the kingis said oratours shall - by the best discrecion they can - enduce thaym of the Hanze to holde thaym content with the provisions and answers geven above or at the lest to put thaym in respit til thair coming into Englande, where shal nough be sette a diete for the same particul poyntis, the perfite conclusion of thies dietee nevertheless fortwith to be taken ... if peradventur the willfulnesse of the Esterlingis at this next diete shal be suche that thay wol have agreed unto thaym thair own provisions in the foresaide poyntis alle or parte of thaym or utterly breke, the kingis said oratours rather than so be breke shal finally under as covert termes as they can

shewe theym condescendable and condescended to that in the said poyntis, withouthe whiche the other partie can not or wol not be enduced agre.'

[9] Barbarossa was able to use the campaign against Henry the Lion (1180/81) to gather Lübeck, hitherto a town belonging to the Welfs, into the imperial fold: Antjekathrin Graßmann (ed.), *Lübeckische Geschichte*, Lübeck 1988, p. 89-91 with Heinrich Appelt et al. (eds.), *Die Urkunden Friedrichs I. (Friderici I. Diplomata)*, 5 vols. (MGH Diplomata regum et imperatorum Germaniae 10/1-5), Hanover 1975-90, vol. 4, N° 981, p. 263-7 (19. Sept. 1188). Frederick II, having granted way the imperial possessions north of the rivers Elbe and Eider to Waldemar II of Denmark in 1214 (Niels Skyum-Nielsen (ed.), *Diplomatarium Danicum, 1. Rœkke, 5. Bind: 1211-1223*, Copenhagen 1957, N° 48, p. 75-79), was able to utilize the war between the Danes and a coalition of North German nobles with Lübeck to regain possession of Lübeck as an imperial town (*Urkundenbuch der Stadt Lübeck*, vol.1, Lübeck 1843, N° 34-5, p. 44-8: cf. Grassmann, *Lübeckische Geschichte*, p. 113-21 with the literature cited on p. 806).

[10] On this subject a convenient summary of the literature may be found in: Stuart Jenks, 'A Capital without a State: Lübeck caput tocius hanze', in: *Historical Research* 65, 1992, p. 134-49, esp. p. 136-9.

[11] This process has been described repeatedly. A convenient summary (with particular reference to the Hanse) may be found in Ahasver von Brandt, *Die Hanse und die nordischen Mächte im Mittelalter* (Arbeitsgemeinschaft für Forschung des Landes Nordrhein-Westfalen Geisteswissenschaften, Heft 102), Cologne/Opladen 1962, reprinted in; Klaus Friedland and Rolf Sprandel (eds.), *Lübeck, Hanse, Nordeuropa. Gedächtnisschrift für Ahasver von Brandt*, Cologne/Vienna 1979, p. 14-36. On the topic in general see Peter Moraw, *Von offener Verfassung zur gestalteten Verdichtung. Das Reich im späten Mittelalter, 1250-1490* (Propläen Geschichte Deutschlands 3), Berlin 1985, p. 149-259, 355-85 (with full bibliography).

[12] von Brandt, *Die Hanse und die nordischen Mächte*, p. 19.

[13] von Brandt, *Die Hanse und die nordischen Mächte*, p. 15.

[14] The phrase was coined by Aksel E. Christensen, *Det nordiske syn på forbindelsen mellem Hansestœderne og Norden*, Aarhus 1957, p. 86, cited from von Brandt, p. 15.

[15] von Brandt, p. 14-17. Cf. Volker Henn, *Was war die Hanse?*, in: Jörgen Bracker et al. (eds.), *Die Hanse. Lebenswirklichkeit und Mythos*. Catalogue of the Hamburg Exposition 1989], Lübeck 1998, p. 14-23.

[16] It should be pointed out that this was characteristic of the relations of all Hanseatic towns trading with England, particularly in the 15th century: Stuart Jenks, *England die Hanse und Preußen: Handel und Diplomatie, 1377-1474* (Quellen und Darstellungen zur Hansischen Geschichte N.S. 38), 3 vols., Cologne/Vienna 1992, vol. 1, p. 444-50.

[17] See Hans van Werveke, 'Der flandrische Eigenhandel im Mittelalter', in: *Hansische Geschichtsblätter 61*, 1936, p. 7-24 and Heinrich Reincke, 'Die Deutschlandfahrt der Flandrer während der hansischen Frühzeit', in: *Hansische Geschichtsblätter* 67/68, 1942/43, p. 51-164.

[18] On this subject see Hugo Stehkämper, 'Friedrich Barbarossa und die Stadt Köln. Ein Wirtschaftskrieg am Niederrhein', in: Hanns Vollrath and Stefan Weinfurter (eds.), *Köln, Stadt und Bistum in Kirche und Reich des Mittelalters. Festschrift für Odilo Engels zum 65. Geburtstag*, Cologne/Weimar/Vienna 1993, p. 367-413, esp. the summary on p. 406-7.

[19] HUB 1.25, p. 16.

[20] HUB 1.14, p. 8. Previous editions of this charter (not to mention Lloyd, *England and the German Hanse*, p. 15) have accepted Lappenberg's erroneous dating (Johann Martin Lappenberg, *Urkundliche Geschichte des hansischen Stahlhofes zu London*, Hamburg 1851, Urkunden N° 2, p. 3-4: '1157'), but Natalie Fryde 'Arnold Fitz Thedmar und die Entstehung der großen deutschen Hanse', in: *Hansische Geschichtsblätter*, 107, 1989, p. 27 with n. 2) was able to demonstrate - by examining when the charter's witnesses obtained and lost their offices - that the document must date from 1175 or 1176. See also Manfred Groten, *Köln im*

13. *Jahrhundert. Gesellschaftlicher Wandel und Verfassungsentwicklung* (Städteforschung Reihe A: Darstellungen, vol. 36), Cologne/Weimar/Vienna 1995, p. 14 and the literature cited there.
[21] HUB 1.13, p. 8. On the dating of this charter see the previous note.
[22] Stehkämper, *Barbarossa und Köln*, p. 390-1.
[23] e.g. in Lynn: HUB 1.116, p. 44 (24 Aug. 1214); HUB 1.160, p. 54 (13 June 1224).
[24] e.g. In Lynn: HUB 1.352, p. 115-6 (1247: Hamburg); HUB 1.364, p. 120 (15 July 1248: Bremen); HUB 1.374, p. 123 (16 May 1249 and 29 May 1250: Staveren).
[25] See Philippe Dollinger, *Die Hanse* (Kröners Taschenbuchausgabe 371), Stuttgart [4]1989, p. 60-2.
[26] In general, see Ellen Wedemeyer Moore, *The Fairs of Medieval England. An Introductory Study* (Studies and Texts 72), Toronto 1985, p. 5. On Lynn in particular as a conduit to the Bury St Edmunds' fairs see Edward Miller and John Hatcher, *Medieval England. Towns, Commerce and Crafts (A Social and Economic History of England)*, London 1995, p. 172, citing Helen M. Cam, *The Eyre of London 14 Edward II A.D. 1321,* 2 vols. (SS 26), London 1968-69, vol. 2, p. 242-3.
[27] Moore, *Fairs*, p. 69ff.
[28] Cf. Dollinger, *Die Hanse,* p. 62ff.
[29] HUB 1.649, S. 223 (28 Dec. 1267).
[30] HUB 1.700-1, S. 246-7 (17 Nov. 1271 and after 28 Feb. 1272).
[31] HUB 1.1036, p. 361-2 (c. 1287).
[32] HUB 2.40, p. 19-22 (15 Aug. 1303).
[33] Norman Scott Brien Gras, *The Early English Customs System. A Documentary Study of the Institutional and Economic History of the Customs from the Thirteenth to the Sixteenth Century,* Cambridge/Mass. 1918, p. 53-8.
[34] Karl Kunze (ed.), *Hanseakten aus England 1275 bis 1412* (Hansische Geschichtsquellen 6), Halle a.S. 1891, N°14, p. 13-5.
[35] HUB 2.40, p. 21.
[36] Arnved Nedkvitne, 'Handelssjøfarten mellom Norge og England I hoymiddelalderen,' in: *Sjøfartshistorisk Årbok. Norwegian Yearbook of Maritime History* 1976 (1977), p. 7-254. For a brief summary of the significance of Nedkvitne's results see Knut Helle, 'Neueste norwegische Forschungen über deutsche Kaufleute' *in Norwegen und ihre Rolle im norwegischen Außenhandel im 12. bis 14.* Jahrhundert, in: *Hansische Geschichtsblätter 98,* 1980, p. 23-38, esp. p. 29-35. Cf. also Arnved Nedkvitne, *Utenrikshandelen fra det vestafjelske Norge 1100-1600,* Bergen 1983 (typescript) p. 33-51, 105-29, 498-502 and 541-2.
[37] e.g. HUB 2.110, S. 46-7 (10 July 1307).
[38] Kunze, *Hanseakten,* N° 32, p. 28. Cf. Moore, *Fairs,* p. 58. Cf. Table 6F, p. 53.
[39] Moore, *Fairs,* p. 204-22.
[40] For a brief summary of these developments see Dorothy M. Owen (ed.), *The Making of King's Lynn. A Documentary Survey* (Records of Social and Economic History N.S. 9), London 1984, p. 47-8.
[41] HUB 2.40, S. 19-22 vom 15.8.1303.
[42] HUB 2.170, p. 74-5 (1 Aug. 1310).
[43] Owen, *Making of King's Lynn,* N° 406 and 408, p. 341-49, 352-62.
[44] The New Custom (*nova custuma*) - agreed between Edward I and the alien merchant community on 1 Feb. 1303 (HUB 2.14 § 10, p. 17-18) - applied only to alien merchandise: Gras, *Customs System,* p.66.
[45] Source: PRO, E122/93/17, edited by Owen, *Making of King's Lynn,* N° 406 and 408, p. 341-49, 352-62.
[46] Not customed by value, but by number.
[47] Not customed by value, but by weight. At this time, a quintal weighed 112 lb.

48 Eleanora M. Carus-Wilson and Olive Coleman (eds.), *England's Export Trade 1275-1547*, Oxford 1963, p. 47, 76, 190.

49 Ibid.

50 HR I.3.319 § 5, p. 316-7.

51 Cf. HUB 4.850, p. 357-8.

52 Stuart Jenks, 'Die Ordnung für die englische Handelskolonie in Danzig (23 Mai 1405)', in: Bernhart Jähnig and Peter Letkemann (eds.), *Danzig in acht Jahrhunderten. Beiträge zur Geschichte eines hansischen und preußischen Mittelpunktes* (Quellen und Darstellungen zur Geschichte Westpreußens 23), Münster 1985, p. 105.

53 1370-88: HR I.3.404, p. 404-16; c. 1388-1436: HR II.2.76, p. 58-76; 1474-91: HR III.2.511, p. 554-63.

54 e.g. KL, C7/3, f.45^v (28 July 1434).

55 KL, C 10/2, f. 50^{iv} (28 Oct. [1480]). Superscription: *De par le roy): Chier et bien ame. Pource qe avant le partir des messages du soverein mestre de Pruce de present esteantz en nostre citee de Loundeos certain traitie se prendra dien devant parentre certains noz commys et deputez dune part et les ditz messages dautre sibien dalliances come de lexcercice de la cours comun de marchandie de chescun coustee, en quell traitie la presence et avis dancins marchantz frequentantz les dictes parties de Pruce sera moult expedient et necessarie, si volus et vous mandons, **qe puisque vous et les autres marchantz de la ville de Lenne meilloure cognoissance avez par experience du fait de marchandie en les parties sus dictes, qe nulls autres marchantz de nostre roiaume,** solez devers nostre counseil en vostres proper persone a Westmonster a toute celeritee possible. Et en cas, qe ce bonement faire ne puerez en vostre dicte persone, facez envore devers nostre dit counsail en toute hast autre marchant de las susdit ville, tiel come bon vous semblera pur besoigner ovesque les ditz messages en le traite susdit selont ce, qe vous ou le dit autre marchant ensorrez a vostre venue depar nous par nostre dit counsail pleinement enfourmez. Et ce en nulle manere ne lessez. Doun souz nostre prive seal a Westmonster, le 28. iour dOctobre.* (my emphasis)

56 HR I.4.350 § 2, p. 339 (15 June 1396). The Prussian towns' complaint was that the English *mit erer koufenschatz dise land* [Prussia] *vorterben und sunderlich mit erem gewande.* For further details see Stuart Jenks, 'Die preußischen Hansestädte und England', in: Zenon Hubert Nowak und Janusz Tandecki (Hgg.), *Die preußischen Städte und ihre Stellung im Nord - und Ostseeraum des Mittelalters* (Ordines Militares - Colloquia Torunensia Historica VIII), Torun 1998, p. 111-129, esp. p. 120-9.

57 HR II.2.221 § 8, p. 178 (May 1438): *das sie so lange mochten hir in den steten und lande wonen, das sie van tage czu tage, van jaren czu jaren, van czeiten czu czeiten hir behusteten und beworczelen mochten und grosse scharen und mennige erer nacien czu sich hir ins landt czyen und holen mochten, das sie durch sulche mennige eres volkes und nacien mochten dis landt und stete undirbrechen und betwingen, alse sie mit sulken listen, bescheidikeit und behendigkeit Bordewes, Garschonien und anir lande undirgebrochen und betwungen hebben.*

58 Cf. Jenks, *England, die Hanse und Preußen*, p. 630-1 et passim.

59 Ibid., p. 485, 489-93, 514, 524, 528, 544, 553, 557, 560, 567, 569, 582, 587, 598, 602, 642-3, 645, 650-1, 662, 666-7, 685, 700, 706, 736, 741.

60 On both subjects, see Jenks, *Die preußischen Hansestädte und England*, esp. p. 123-5.

61 This was stated explicitly by the Prussian ambassador Arnt van Dassel in a letter to the Prussian towns on 25 Jan. 1409 (HR I.5.548, p. 441): *...Ok geleve juwer wysheit to weten, dat to London is gekomen Brandon, Jon Brun und andere borgere van Linden, de geven my guden trost unde zegghen, dat ik unvorvart sy, ik sulle een gud antwerde hebben van allen mynen saken, yd gha welken wech, dat yd gha. Unde dat meenen sealdus vort to bringen, dat se dem rade van Engelant clagen willen ere not, dat ys all umme korne, und zegghen, dat in der nortkost alle dat korne vorloren sy, unde id is zune dure tiid in dessem lande to werden. Unde se willen dem rade byllen upsteken, unde clagen, ys dat sake, dat my nicht een gud antwerde wert, so sy alle ere trost vorloren, den se to dem lande van Prussen hebben, want se gheen lant en weten, dar se korne ut hebben mogen, denn ut*

Prussen. On John Broun as Lynn's representative at these talks see KL C10/2 f. 38ᵛ. In 1408 or early 1409 (prior to 25 Jan.), Lynn also petitioned the Council to make peace with Prussia, particularly in view of the scarcity of grain in England (KL C10/2 f. 27ᵛ-28ʳ. Superscription: *Copia bille in Gallica lingua recitande voluntatem Regis, ut patet): Supplient treshumblement lez marchauntz dEngleterre usauntz et conversauntz lez parties de Pruce, qe come nostre tressoverain seignur le roy ore tarde envoia par Arnold de Dasshell messages del haut mestre de Pruce ces tresgraciouses letters directez au dit haut mestre contenauntz leffeit de relacion et report des matiers de reparacion parentre nostre dit seignur le roy et ses lieges et le dit mestre et ses subgitz, sur quex letters suisditz le dit message depuis ad appert et delivere a nostre dit tresexcellent seignur le roy letters des respounse, sur qoi la volunte de nostre dit tresgracious seignur le roy et, qe sibien sez letters suisditz come les suisditz letters toutpuissailles fuissent veies et declares paredevaunt soun tressage consaille, au fin qils puissant ester my en exploit solonc la tenure et purport decelle. Pur quoy plese a voz tresnobles seignuries et tressagez discreceons considerer le graund escarciete et chierte de frument et autres bledz ore encurruz en iceste roialme et le beal plenite des bledz en les parties de Pruce et comment iceux de Pruce ne violent suffrer en nulle manere de passer hors de lours parties de venir en nulle maners parties deceste roialme nulle bledz ne nulle marchaunt diceste roialme nose oventurer nulle maners marchaundises de passer en les parties de Pruce, avaunt qe la matier suisdit soit mys en exploit. Et sur ceo vous plese al reverence de Dieux par voz tressagez et treshautz avys ordeigner, qe la matier avauntdit soit mys en exploit et qe letters de respounse roialx soient en celle partie envoies a dit haut mestre de Pruce, par ensi qe bon accorde, tranquillite et unite finalment puisse ester fait entre iceste roialme et iceux de Pruce pur Dieux et en oevere de charite, considerauntz tresgracious seignure, qe, si le dit matere ne soit mys en hastyf expoit, il serra graund damage sibien en la custume nostre dit seignur le roy et en distruccioun del navoie de sa roialme come en outré diffesaunces et anientisment dez plusours ses poveres lieges, qe Dieu ne veulle.*

⁶² The letter of Danzig's representative Heinrich Vorrat to Danzig (HR II.2.65, p. 45-8, 12 Dec. 1436, here p. 45) speaks volumes: *Ok bringen de van Linden, Hul und andere ut der nortcost, de in Prusen plegen [to] vorkeren und den unsen meist unrechtes und schaden hebben gedan, so vel unredeliker logenhaftige gedichte und clage vor, meist up myn herren homeister und ju herren [viz. the Town Council of Danzig], ok up ander stede, darmede se so vel hindernis uns hebben gedan, dat dar to vel van were to schriven.*

⁶³ Treaty of London: HR II.2.84, p. 84-8 (for its interpretation cf. Jenks, *England, die Hanse und Preußen*, p. 600-17). On the English (particularly from Lynn, Hull and Boston) taking advantage of the commercial opportunities which opened up see HR II.2.70, p. 51-3.

⁶⁴ HR II.2.84 § 2, p. 85 (English in Prussia) and § 4, p. 85 (Hanse merchants in England).

⁶⁵ HR II.2.84 § 1, p. 85. § 3, p. 85 specifically prohibited the collection of subsidies (of which tunnage and poundage were but two) from Hanse merchants in England.

⁶⁶ Note, for instance, the wording of § 1, p. 85, which stipulated that all English merchants and subjects were free to visit Prussia and other Hanseatic towns and there *omnibus et singulis illis liberatibus et liberis consuetudinibus uti plene debeant et gaudere, quibus **unquam aliquo tempore racionabiliter** usi sunt et gavisi* (my emphasis).

⁶⁷ Jenks, *England, die Hanse und Preußen*, p. 631-55.

⁶⁸ HR II.2.222, p. 178-9 (12 May 1438); HR II.2.223 § 1, p. 179-80 (12 May 1438); Thomas Rymer (ed.), *Foedera, conventions, litterae et cujuscunque generis acta publica inter reges Angliae et alios quosvis imperatores, reges, pontifices vel communitates (1101-1654)*, 10 vols, The Hague ²1739-45, vol. 5/1, p. 72 (2 Feb. 1440); HR II.2.346, p. 281 (c. 2 Feb. 1440); HR II.2.380, p. 304-5 (14 July 1440). Thereafter, complaints about this matter died down, as the High Master had agreed to the abolition of poundage in Prussia (*Pfundzoll*) in May 1440: Jürgen Sarnowsky, *Die Wirtschaftsführung des Deutschen Ordens in Preußen (1382-1454)* (Veröffentlichungen aus den Archiven Preußischer Kulturbesitz 34), Cologne/Weimar/Vienna 1993, p. 75.

[69] Jenks, *England, die Hanse und Preußen*, p. 469-70 and 622-3 with graphs 15, p. 277, 17, p. 284 and 31, p. 470.

[70] Jenks, *Die preußischen Hansestädte und England*, p. 127-9.

[71] Trade figures: Jenks, *England die Hanse und Preußen*, p. 417-20 and 1018-24. Capture of the salt fleet returning from the Baie de Bourgneuf (near Nantes) on 23 May 1449: ibid, p. 667-8.

[72] HR II.2.536, p. 405-6 (18 July 1449).

[73] Paul Simson, *Geschichte der Stadt Danzig bis 1626*, 3 vols., Danzig 1913, ND Aalen 1967, vol. 3, N° 141, p. 114-8.

[74] e.g. HUB 8.574, p. 377-8 (28 May 1457); HUB 8.754, p. 469 (Dec. 1458).

[75] Jenks, *Die preußischen Hansestädte und England*, Graph 2, p. 115.

[76] Among other things, the Anglo-Danish treaty of 3 Oct. 1465 had made sailing to Iceland dependent upon obtaining a licence from the King of Norway: Absalon Taranger et al. (eds.), *Norges gamle love. Anden række 1388-1604*, 2 vols., Christiania 1912-34, vol. 2, part 1: *Statens lovgivning*, N° 100, p. 155-9. On English trade with Iceland in general see Eleanora M. carus-Wilson, 'The Iceland Venture', in: Eadem, *Medieval Merchant Venturers. Collected Studies*, London 1954, p. 98-142. On Lynn's trade with Iceland cf. Eadem, *The Medieval Trade of the Ports of the Wash*, in: *Medieval Archaeology* 6/7, 1962/3, p. 182-201, here p. 199-200.

[77] KL C7/2, p. 247-8 (printed - with a considerable number of transcription errors - by Alexander Bugge, *Diplomatarium Norwegicum*, vol. 19, Christiania 1910, p. 49), dated 13 May 1429 (Superscription: *Congregacio tenta ibidem 13° die Maij anno suprascripto [7 Henry VI]; marginalized p. 248 Restrictio navigacionis versus Islandiam):Et ibidem querela facta fuit pro navigacione versus Islandiam, eo quod timendum est, ut rex Dacie eos versus Pruciam et Norberne velantes arrestari faciat bona sua. Ad quod responderunt T. Wilkynson, Willelmus Kirtone et Johannes Stantone et pecierunt, ut habeant licenciam pro anno isto et decetero nolunt usitare. Et multa dicta fuerunt, eo quod fecerunt contra ordinancionem ville expresse, prout eis manifeste declaratum sub communi sigillo remanente in thesauro. Super quo ipsi T. et Willelmus aulam exierunt. Et tunc congragacio consuluit, quid esset faciendum, et exivit eciam cum eis Johannes Kaarle et Willelmus Kirtone. Et postea intraverunt T. Wilkynson et Johannes Stantone, et pet[i] tum fuit eis per majorem, si voluerint dimittere eorum navigacionem versus Islandiam ad presens. Et concesserunt dimittere et navigare usque Norberne, ita quod eorum attornati, cum ibidem veniunt in Norberne, sic tractentur in omnibus, sicut ipsi, qui Norberne visitati fuerunt et eadem mercatam usitati sunt. --- Cf. also KL C7/2 p. 253 (Superscription: Congregacio omnium mercatorum Lenne tenta die Veneris 17° die Junit anno [7 Henry VI]. Marginalized: Electio personarum a[d] transmittendum regi Dacie): Et ibidem mota fuit per majorem, quoniam rumores de Fflandria advenerunt, quoniam naves de Lenne carcate ad Pruciam transmisse per regem Dacie sunt arrestate, quid in hac parte erit faciendum. Et concordati sunt in hunc modum, quod duo erunt electi de burgensibus ad mittendum eidem regi. Et vocatus est pro electione:Willelmus Style, Johannes Brekeroppe, Thomas Worsted, Johannes Waryne. Qui vocaverunt ad see: Ricardum Letthour, Johannem Brightyene, Johannem Gedeneye, Willelmum Kirtone. Qui vocaverunt: Johannem Dune, Johannem Assende, Willelmum Raulyne, Willelmum Style juniorem. Et antequam dicti electi aliquos nominaverunt, tota congregacio concessit, ut si quis electus fuerit et recusaverit transire, solvet £20 ad dictum usum convertendum. Et ipsi sic electi habebunt pro eorum labore ultra expensas suas juxta discrecionem electionis. Et postea elegerunt T[homam] Salisbury et habebit pro suo regardo £20. Et Johannem Pygot et habebit pro suo regardo £15. Qui quidem Thomas ipsum excusavit racione senectutis patris et matris eius, quorum onus custodie in se suscepit.*

[78] Carus-Wilson, *Iceland Venture*, p. 138.

[79] To wit *le James de Lynne* (owners: Richard Outlaw, Edmund Westthorp, Richard Goodwyn and Thomas Leighton) and the balenger *le Marye de Lynne* (owners Richard Outlaw and Alan Thomson; skipper Robert Deryng of Lynn).

[80] The ensuing arrest of the Hanseatic merchants in England and their subsequent trial threw up a massive documentation (necessarily subjective in tone) on the incident. For the original petition of complaint and the depositions of the English victims see HUB 9.478, p. 331-3 and HUB 9.519, p. 364-8 respectively.

[81] HR II.6.111, p. 85, daten 29 Sept. 1468.

[82] The *Valentyne of Newecastell* (or of *Hull*): HUB 9.519 § 15-19, p. 368. See also the complaint of John Nevill, Earl of Northumberland, on the capture of the *Valentyne*: HUB 9.520, p. 520-1 (Oct.-21 Nov. 1468).

[83] The order to arrest the Hanseatic merchants dates from 28 July 1468: HUB 9.480, p. 335. On the Nevills' role see Ross, *Edward IV*, p. 121, 311, 365-6. The point was not lost on the London Steelyard: HR II.6.97, p. 71-3, here p. 73.

[84] HUB 9.478, p. 331-3.

[85] For the *disputation* of the estimable Dr Johannes Osthusen see HUB 9.584, p. 462-74. The Dean of the Lübeck cathedral chapter was concerned to rebut the charges made by Edward IV's Roman lawyers, who sought to justify the actions of the English government: HUB 9.570, p. 453-7. For the efforts of the London Steelyard on its own behalf see Stuart Jenks, 'Die Hansen in England. Die wirtschaftliche und politische Bedeutung ihres Handels (1380-1474) und ihre Versuche zur Bewältigung der Krise von 1468', in: Volker Henn and Arnved Nedkvitne (eds.), *Norwegen und die Hanse. Wirtschaftliche und kulturelle Aspekte im europäischen Vergleich* (Kieler Werkstücke, Reihe A, vol. 11), Frankfurt 1994, p. 109-59, esp. p. 137-52.

[86] HUB 9.527, p. 382-3. All Cologne merchants were acquitted and released from prison on 26 Nov. 1468: HUB 9.528, p. 383.

[87] HR II.6.184 § 48-9, p. 154. Cf. Danzig's suggestion that a prohibition of the import of English cloth would bring about the release of the imprisoned Hanseatic merchants: HR II.6.161, p. 123-4 (6 Feb. 1469).

[88] HUB 9.585, p. 474 (17 May 1469).

[89] Danzig demanded the outfitting of ships against England on 26 Dec. 1469 (HR II.6.283, p. 263-5). Cf. However Hamburg's answer of 19 Jan. 1470 (HR 2.6.285, p. 265-6) and Danzig's response of 14 Apr. 1470 (HR II.6.289, p. 267). Danzig sent ships to fight against England and France on 28 Apr. 1470 (HR II.6.314, p. 276). However, the Bruges factory had initiated hostilities against England in the autumn of 1469 without waiting for a formal declaration of war by the Diet: Theodor HIRSCH (ed.), *Caspar Weinreichs Danziger Chronik* in: Idem (ed.), *Scriptores rerum Prussicarum. Die Geschichtsquellen der preußischen Vorzeit bis zum Untergange der Ordensherrschaft*, vol. 4, Leipzig 1870, p. 731: *Item diesen herbest* [1469] *war zu rath der kofman zu Brugge und ander gutte gesellen und kofleute und reideden etliche schiffe ausz auff dieEnglischen und Frantzen zur oreley bey namen Paul Beneke und Merten Bardewigk und etliche andere etc.*

[90] On the course of the war (in which neither side was able to gain a decisive advantage) see Jenks, *England, die Hanse und Preußen*, p. 731-3.

[91] HR II.7.34 § 51, p. 34: *nademe de von Londen unde mer stede in Engelland desses kriges unde mishegelicheyd zere weren orsake.*

[92] HR II.7.34 § 43, § 45, p. 32-3 (Hanseatic report on the negotiations in Utrecht); HUB 10.241 § 40, p. 149 (report of the English delegates in Utrecht): 'Bout above this for the harmes and rebukes that Londoners and other Englisch men had doon unto thaim, they wold have of fre yifte delivered unto thaim the Stilyerd in London, oon house in Boston, another in Lynne'. HUB 10.241 § 40, p. 149: 'As to the second point of the Styleyerd and other howses thay said that all London did thaim right grete injuries and rebukes, rehersing that at beginning of the kinges reign thay wer the letters that the king confermed not their privileges. Thay also putte a bill into the parlement for to lette the said confirmacion. Also thay have constreyned hem many years to pay thaim 32 nobles yearly without eny reasonable or righwise cause. Also wher thay be privileged that thay shuld paye no prestes, taxes ne other

graunte to the king, the Londoners nathelesse compelled thaim to diverse contribucions, wherfor they aske the said howse' (§ 42, p. 150).

[93] This is emphasized in the Peace of Utrecht: HR II.7.142 § 8, p. 344-5:'*Item appunctuatum, conventum, concordatum et conclusum est, quod serenissimus dominus rex Anglie ad uberiorem satisfaccionem et recompensam omnium et singulorum dampnorum, injuriarum et contumeliarum, de quibus per subditos corone Anglie hominibus Hanze factis et perpetratis multipliciter querulatum est, preter et ultra alias recompenses quascumque concordatas et advisatas* [sc. compensation of £10,000: ibid. § 9, p. 345-6], *certas domos et mansiones eis et eorum successoribus imperpetuum possidendas et habendas appropriabit seu appropriari faciet, videlicet quondam curiam London' sitam, vocatam Staelhoeff alias Stieljerd, cum eidem adherentibus edificiis et ejusdem universis juribus usque ad Guildehaldam Theutonicorum inclusive se extendentem; item in villa de Boston curiam de Staelhoeff, alias dictam Stiljerd, et quod in villa de Lenna una domus consimilis pro usu et utilitate dictorum mercatorum Hanze juxta aquas ordinetur ac similiter per eundem dominum regem eis et eorum sucessoribus imperpetuum possidenda approprietur*'.

[94] On such expiatory gestures see Stuart Jenks, 'Friedensvorstellungen der Hanse (1356-1474)', in: Johannes Fried (Hg.), *Träger und Instrumentarien des Friedens im hohen und späten Mittelalter* (Vorträge und Forschungen 43), Sigmaringen 1996, p. 405-39, here p. 429-39.

[95] HR II.7.184, p. 394-5.

[96] HUB 10.477 § 57, p. 306.

[97] On Patenmaker's relations with Gerhard von Wesel, Alderman of the London Steelyard, during the crisis of 1468 see HUB 9.535, p. 398 (30 Dec. 1468). For Wright see HUB 9.548, p. 431 and 541 X § 11, p. 424.

[98] John D. Fudge, *Cargoes, Embargoes, and Emissaries. The Commercial and Political Interaction of England and the German Hanse, 1450-1510*, Toronto 1995, p. 100. Cf; T.H. Lloyd, *England and the German Hanse, 1157-1611. A Study of their Trade and Commercial Diplomacy*, Cambridge 1991, p. 285-6.

[99] HUB 10.241 § 40, p. 149, § 75, p. 158 (20 July 1473); cf. the report of the Hanseatic delegates: HR II.7.34 § 43, p. 32-3, § 48, p. 33-4 and § 106, p. 47-8.

[100] Cf. the demands of the Hanseatic delegation of 27 July 1473 (HR II.7.37 § 28, p. 98-9): '*et in Lienden consimilem curiam prope aquas*'.

[101] '*...in villa de Lenne una domus consimilis pro usu et utilitate dictorum mercatorum Hanze in quadam platea vulgariter nuncupata Cheker, juxta aquas:*' HR II.7.44 § 12, p. 125.

[102] Vanessa Parker, *The Making of King's Lynn. Secular Buildings from the 11th to the 17th Century* (King's Lynn Archaeological Survey vol. 1), London and Chichester 1971, p. 36, 38, 43. See also the illustration showing Lynn's waterfront c. 1730 in Paul Richards, *King's Lynn,* Chichester 1990, ND 1997, p. 20 (ill. 8).

[103] Parker, *Making of King's Lynn*, p. 42.

[104] HR II.7.34 § 46, p.33.

[105] HR II.7.34 § 48, p. 33-4 (21 July 1473).

[106] HR II.7.34 § 44, p. 33 (20 July 1473) and § 106, p. 47-8 (6 Sept. 1473).

[107] HR II.7.34 § 76, p. 158.

[108] HR II.7.107 § 8, p. 214-5: 'Item as touching the 12. article for the appropriacion of certain houses in London, Boston and Lynne to the merchauntis of the Hanse, the king is content that his oratours passé and conclude with the oratours of the same Hanse worde for worde, as the same article importeth, excepte this worde 'Cheker' concernyng the hous in Lynne, onlesse than they can obteyn any better or esier way, excepte that the shal have noo act of parliament theruppon, like as it is not necessarye to have. And if they think that the verry transport and appropriacion shuld have be made tham of the premises now forthwith, thay shal say that it could not be so nor yitte hit was not accorded so to be doon at the last departing of the oratours of both sydis, but oonly the oratoures to have power to conclude and to conclude upon alle that was appooynted betweyn them at the rathe diete, as hit

113

appereth by the 34. article. And as for the time that shal be apponyted al this to be perfourmed, thay shal accorde to half a yere or to a yere'.

[109] HR II.7.138 § 24, p. 248.

[110] HR II.7.142 § 8, p. 344-5: *'certas domos et mansiones eis et eorum successoribus imperpetuum possidendas et habendas appropriabit seu appropriari faciet, videlicet quondam curiam London' sitam, vocatam Staelhoeff alias Stieljerd, cum eidem adherentibus edificiis et ejusdem universis juribus usque ad Guildehaldam Theutonicorum inclusive se extendentem; item in villa de Boston cuiam de Staelhoeff, alias dictam Stiljerd, et quod in villa de Lenna una domus consimilis pro usu et utilitate dictorum mercatorum Hanze juxta aquas ordinetur ac similiter per eundem dominum regem eis et eorum successoribus imperpetuum possidenda approprietur'.* Note that all the verbs relating to the London and Boston Steelyards are in the future, but those relating to the Lynn house are in the subjunctive.

[111] KL, C7/4 f. 158ᵛ (p. 317). This is confirmed by a letter which the Hanseatic delegates Herman Wanmate and Arnd Winkenson wrote to the Bruges factory: on the 4th of November the king had informed them that he had summoned representatives of Boston and Lynn before the council in order to clarify the question of the houses to be granted to the Hanse and expected the representatives of the towns named to be in Westminster in five or six days: HR II.7.103, p. 203-5 (12 Nov. 1473).

[112] Leighton and Thoresby had received a safe conduct from Danzig in 1457 (HUB 8.574, p. 377-8), and somewhat later Thoresby bought a Prussian ship there (HUB 8.639, p. 412). Wales was called to testify about the seizure of the English ships in the Sound in 1468 (HUB 519 § 3, p. 365 and 521 § 2, p. 371). Together with another Lynn merchant, Henry Bermyngham, Cony had been named to the delegation which negotiated with the Hanse in Hamburg in 1465 (HR II.6.540, p. 416; 654, p. 463; 667, p. 466; 712, p. 480).

[113] Leighton owned part of the ship *James de Lynn* which was seized (HUB 9.478, p. 332); For Wales cf. HUB 9.519 § 3, p. 365 and 521 § 2, p. 271.

[114] HUB 9.541 IV § 2, p. 414; X § 2 & 11, p. 423-4.

[115] Owen, *Making of King's Lynn*, p. 28.

[116] AHL Anglicans 209 (copy: PRO, C66/535 m 6; calendared in HUB 10.411, p. 255): the property in question, formerly owned by Philip With, was described as lying *'exopposito ecclesie sancta Margarete ejusdem ville inter vicum regium ibidem ex parte orientali et communem aquam dicte ville de Lenne ex parte occidentali et tenementum quondam Johannis Lakynghithe postea* **Johannis Thorysby** *ex parte boriali et tenementum nuper Roberti att Lathe ex parte oustrali'* (my emphasis).

[117] Parker, *Making of King's Lynn*, p. 70-1 and plate 13B; Richards, *King's Lynn*, p. 60, ill. 24.

[118] HUB 9.473, p. 329 (8 July 1468). It is worth mentioning in this context that the clerk whom John Maldone of London charged with conducting the conveyance for him, one Nicholas Enmeth (HUB 9, p. 329 n. 1: note that Enmeth's name is erroneously transcribed there), was parochial chaplain of St. Margaret's in 1479 (Owen, *Making of King's Lynn*, Nᵒ 474, p. 429).

[119] Fudge, *Cargoes*, p. 98-102, 155-60, 163.

The plaque in the courtyard of the Hanseatic Steelyard at King's Lynn
presented by
His Excellency the German Ambassador Gebhardt von Moltke
6th June 1998.

The text is also given below to ensure legibility.

THE HANSEATIC LEAGUE

*This union of German medieval towns was a major influence in the
commerce of northern Europe from around 1200 and created a whole
network of trading posts abroad, of which this complex of buildings is the
only one still preserved in England. It was assigned to the Hanseatic
League by Edward IV in 1475.
The German merchants departed in 1571 and the property was leased to
local merchants until it was sold by the Mayor of Lübeck for £800 in 1751
to Edward Everard, who rebuilt the street range.
St Margaret's House is the name now given to these historic buildings,
which were restored by Norfolk County Council in 1971.*

*Presented by His Excellency the German Ambassador
Gebhardt von Moltke 6th June 1998*

FESTIVAL ADDRESS

June 6, 1998

H.E. the Ambassador of the Federal Republic of Germany

Dr iur. h.c. Gebhardt v. Moltke

Mr Mayor (Dr Paul Richards), Honorary Consul (Mr David W. Hume), Ladies and Gentlemen,

We have gathered today to unveil this plaque in commemoration of the Hanseatic League and the part it played in the history of the economic development of this part of England.

It is very gratifying to consider the contribution made by those historic trading links to the early prosperity of this region of England and the importance of King's Lynn, former Bishop's Lynn, once fourth largest English town. Those links were a first step not only towards the intensive trade relations that exist today, but also to cultural, architectural and many other ties between our two countries and those around the North Sea.

In those days travelling overseas was a hazardous undertaking, with the weather conditions playing a decisive role for the success of a trade mission. All the more we admire the establishment of a whole network of trading posts in Northern Europe by the Hanseatic League. The main tasks of these trading posts were – quite similar by the way to what Embassies are engaged in nowadays – permanent representation to safeguard their interests, consular protection and trade promotion. Another reason was, not surprisingly, to unite in order to negotiate free trade zones.

In that sense, they may be considered as fathers of what one could call an early European Economic Community. Here, in King's Lynn, they found a very active port and trading post to which their warehouses testify still today.

I wonder whether our ancestors of that time could have imagined the degree to which European countries today are interlinked both economically and culturally, are part of a European Union, or that indeed Britain would be connected with continental Europe by a tunnel! Had they known, they might have tried to keep this wonderful building which is now St Margaret's House.

Winds of history were changing in the 16th century and brought an end to the Hanseatic involvement in English trade. Before the Hanseatic League had to leave England, it entertained a number of posts and warehouses along England's east coast: here in King's Lynn, in York, Hull, Boston, Yarmouth, Ipswich and London. This building in front of us, however, is the only reminder of the time, the only Hanseatic League building that has survived changes of history.

May it be for many more years to come not only a symbol of the commercial relations of the past, but also a forward-looking encouragement for people from our two countries to meet and build the common future together. The best example is certainly today's symposium with so many guests from Germany and other countries and which the Mayor, Dr Paul Richards, has so splendidly organized.

I am very pleased to unveil this commemorative plaque here today as a living symbol of an outgoing millennium, a millennium of economic and cultural links of our nations.

Let us raise our glass to that!

PARTICIPANTS

Dr Barbara Brodt	German Historical Institute London, England
Prof. Dr Detlev Ellmers	Bremerhaven, Germany
Prof. Dr Klaus Friedland	Heikendorf, Germany
Prof. Eva Friedland	
Dr Antjekathrin Graßmann	Lübeck, Germany
Prof. Dr habil. Andrzej Groth	Gdynia, Poland
Dr Elisabeth Heinsius	Mölln, Germany
Prof. Dr Stuart Jenks	Fürth, Germany
Prof. Dr Kurt Jürgensen	Kronshagen, Germany
Ingeborg Jürgensen	
Dr Klaus Krüger	Jena, Germany
Stud. Dir. a. D. Günter Meyer	Malente, Germany
Prof. Dr Walter Salmen	Kirchzarten, Germany
Dr Gabriele Busch-Salmen	
Prof. Dr Walter Stark	Greifswald, Germany
Dr Hugo Weczerka	Marburg, Germany
Elisabeth Weczerka	
Bärbl Wirrer, MA	Spenge, Germany

ENGLISH PARTICIPANTS

Dr Abulafia	Cambridge University
Dr John Alban	Norfolk Record Office
Brian Ayres	Norfolk Archaeological Unit
Dr John Barney	Norwich
Michael Begley	King's Lynn
Alison Gifford	
Susan Maddock	Norfolk Record Office
Dr Alan Metters	Norwich City College
Patricia Midgley	True's Yard Museum
David Victor Proctor	Rochester
Dr Paul Richards	King's Lynn, England
Mayor of King's Lynn & West Norfolk	
Dr Ann Robey	Royal Commission on Historical Monuments of England
Syd Swan	Suffolk